Operate, Operate, Operate!

A young surgeon in the 1970s

By

Douglas MacMillan

Table of Contents

Dedication

Oriana

About the Author

Douglas MacMillan qualified in medicine at St. Thomas' Hospital, London, in 1966 and, after discarding his first intention of being an obstetrician and gynaecologist, specialised in Ear, Nose, and Throat surgery. Recent reading in both the popular press and surgical journals suggests that many young doctors are discounting a career in surgery because of hard work, long working hours, and a poor work/life balance. This book was written to retaliate against these claims: although a surgeon in his retirement may be accused of viewing the past through rose-tinted spectacles, there is little doubt that we thoroughly enjoyed ourselves, working hard (ridiculously so in some cases) and playing hard (in most cases). Work/life balance? As surgeons we just wanted to operate, operate, and operate…

This little book gives a picture of the formative years of a junior doctor in the early 1970s, hopefully illuminating the joy of being a surgeon, the style of medical practice fifty years ago, and – more significantly – remembering many patients who influenced and informed Douglas' philosophy of life.

Music has played a fundamental part of Douglas' life alongside (and almost threatening to displace) his surgical career. His retirement has been devoted to the study of musical instruments and he is the proud possessor doctorates in music from the University of Oxford and the Royal

College of Music – and, lest we forget, he is also a Fellow of the Royal College of Surgeons of England…

Prelude

In recent years much has been written in both the medical and the popular press about a shortage of doctors, and much ink has been spilt trying to contextualise this dilemma which, after all, potentially affects every man, woman, and child on the planet. No matter where you fit into the social pile, you are liable to suffer an illness, and even royalty and billionaires are not immune to disease.

The real reason that I put pen to paper to write this small book is that I am both concerned about and angry with junior doctors who do not want to become surgeons, often citing long hours, intensive study, bullying, and a career that is a threat to their work/life balance. As a retired ENT surgeon in his eightieth year, I formed the opinion that someone should write about his own enjoyable and stimulating time as a junior doctor and surgical trainee in the late 1960s and early 1970s. I hope I shall not be accused of being a dinosaur and viewing the past through rose-tinted spectacles, but I do believe we enjoyed our work despite absurdly long hours, not the greatest of salaries, and the ever-present threat of failing to make the grade. We worked hard, but we played hard – in the very supportive 'family' environment of the traditional firm of consultant, registrar, and houseman. With the collapse of this time-honoured hierarchy, shorter working hours, and the emergence of the shift system consequent upon the European Working Time Directive, much of the unwritten and unrecognised advantage of a supportive medical hierarchy has sadly been lost – as has much of the trainer/trainee relationship.

The few names cited in the book have been changed but with the notable exception of Harold, who I thought justified his own honourable mention. 'The boss' could refer to any one of the twenty-odd consultants for whom I worked, but it is only fitting to pay tribute to Robin McNab Jones at Barts and Peter Milling at University College Hospital. Both men could only be described as formative in my training: both were elegant surgeons and shrewd clinicians. To them, I owe deep gratitude.

Medical Student

As a fourteen-year-old pupil at Wycliffe College (we were not 'students' at school in those far-off days), I was summoned to the Headmaster's study not, I hasten to add, for any misdemeanour but to determine whether I should take an arts or science pathway. I was asked if I had any thoughts on a career, and, for some inexplicable reason, I said, 'I thought I might read medicine, Sir'. To this day, I do not know what prompted this response: I do not come from a medical family, but I think I was rather impressed by the exploits of the flamboyant surgeon Sir Lancelot Spratt (played by James Robertson Justice) in the *Doctor in the House* movies of the late 1950s. I applied to St. Thomas' Hospital Medical School (it had a nice cream prospectus with an embossed coloured crest) and was summoned for an interview. We talked about my interest in rowing and sailing, after which the Dean said, 'But don't you play any football games?' – hardly an unexpected comment from an institution that prided itself on its rugby team. When I had blurted out my honest answer, 'only when I have to, Sir,' I thought my chances of a place were slim.

Nevertheless, in October 1960, I arrived at that august (and pompous) institution, clutching my Gray's anatomy. My diary recorded my first impressions: 1. hard work 2. boring hard work.

This book does not set out to be a catalogue of the trials and tribulations of being a medical student, but I think I should note that I found the whole process rather uninspiring from an intellectual point of view. I am very much a polymath with an overriding interest in music, the arts, and philosophical theology and was bitterly disappointed to find that the Medical School Library contained only medical books. I should have gone to Oxford, but that had to wait until I could read for a DPhil at the age of 72!

Somehow or other, I eventually persuaded the examiners that I knew enough about medicine to be awarded the degrees of Bachelor of Medicine and Bachelor of Surgery and was fit to set out on a career healing the sick and earning a respectable (about £14,000 in today's money) salary. I was given no career advice: the rugby players all got house jobs, but second clarinettists were not on the priority list for employment at Thomas's. I ploughed into the *British Medical Journal* and applied for a house physician post in Brighton: it looked like a nice place by the sea, not too far from civilisation (London), and, as an aspiring surgeon, I thought I would get the medical job out of the way before attending to my career proper as a surgical trainee. My initial aspiration was to be an obstetrician and gynaecologist (one of the few firms I had enjoyed as a student), but I had also developed an interest in ENT. I never wanted to be a physician, let alone a psychiatrist…

But more of this later: in May 1966, I took the train to Brighton, my luggage containing the basic necessities of life, including a stethoscope, some medical textbooks, and my treble recorder.

Chapter 1

House Physician

(or what is now called Foundation Year 1) Brighton General Hospital

And so, on a May afternoon in 1966, I took a taxi from Brighton Station to K Block, the doctors' mess at Brighton General Hospital. Brighton General was a rambling Victorian creation perched on a hill beside the racecourse, with blocks containing wards (mine were E2 and E3 – not very imaginative names!), administrators (whom I was trained to view with scorn), a laundry, a path lab, and the doctors' mess in K block. We worked to a 1 in 2 or 1 in 3 rota, so most of the twelve or so of us were resident: the mess was the centre of our lives, where we ate, slept, socialised, and bonded as a community of young doctors.[1]

I had rocked up on a propitious day – a mess dinner, presided over by the Mess President, a Very Senior Man who was a very talented Senior House Officer in surgery. Nobody had any concerns about a drink or two when on duty (and it was just pre-breathalyser…), and I applied the letters 'TTO' not always to patient's drugs 'to take out' on discharge, but to a few bottles brought back from the pub for those who were on call. An overpowering memory of how

[1] Monday off: Tuesday on: Wednesday off (half day): Thursday on: Friday, Saturday Sunday on, with the other house physician taking this rota on the next week. 'Off' means a normal day's work on the wards (0830–*c*1800) but not 'on take' for emergencies.

well we were respected and treated was Dot's question each morning as I appeared for breakfast in the mess 'one egg or two, Dr MacMillan'.

New doctor

After years at medical school, I had acquired enough knowledge of medicine to be provisionally registered with the General Medical Council to work under supervision in a hospital. Sure, I knew a lot about medicine and about drugs, but I had not the slightest idea of how to be a doctor: it was one thing as a final year student to be asked by one's teacher 'what would *you* do?' and being at a bedside at three in the morning thinking 'what (the xxx!) am *I* going to do?' On my first evening, I was asked to prescribe night sedation for a patient: I wrote the date at one end of the line, my signature at the end, and turned to the staff nurse, 'what do I put in the middle?' I could easily reel off the pharmacological properties of the drugs, but I had no knowledge of how to write a prescription. I had never set up an intravenous infusion (a drip), although I could whip a toenail off! These technical skills were easily learnt, but we had received absolutely no training in how to talk to patients, how to convey bad news, or how to deal with anxious relatives – or, indeed, with ward sisters. Partly, I suspect, that this was a problem of the generation, although I am not convinced that the juniors are that much better at it nowadays despite the training they apparently receive in such matters. Also, I think we must recall that doctors could be incredibly high-handed, unempathetic, unsympathetic, and expected to be accorded a status not far below the divine. I recall one senior surgeon standing at the end of a patient's bed and announcing, 'you have an ulcer. I'll cut out your stomach next week'… Not exactly informed consent, as the lawyers would accept it today, but it passed for the norm half a century ago. It is perhaps little wonder that the most impressive figure I encountered as an undergraduate was Dame Cicely Saunders, the founder of palliative care medicine. *She cared.*

But I digress: new doctors were given much more responsibility and independence than the FY1 doctors of today: we had work to do, and plenty of it. We two house physicians were responsible for 60 medical beds, supervised by a registrar who was not prone to decision-making, so we just got on with it. In those far-off days, we had enormous responsibility placed on our immature shoulders, for we were the first in line to care for heart attacks, strokes, acute stomach bleeds, severe asthmatics and diabetic crises. There is no doubt that the learning curve was almost vertical, but it was both a huge challenge and huge fun, despite the inevitable moments of doubt, perplexity, and fear. I don't think I actually killed anyone… By the way, we had no bleeps: the call system was a series of flashing numbers in each place where doctors might be found. My number was 4224, and when I was 'flashed'(!) I would call a very efficient and seemingly all-knowing telephone switchboard for further instructions. And, please note in these days when casual dress is required because of a brainless government decree, that we looked like doctors in our white coats; one friend of mine who was 'on the house' at another hospital kept a silver hip-flask of brandy in her white coat pocket, but most us just carried a stethoscope, notebooks, and, for some, a packet of cigarettes.

The hierarchy

A Professor of Surgery is reputed to have greeted his new firm of students with a short address. 'Medicine is like an enormously high mountain. I am right at the top, and you, ladies and gentlemen, ARE RIGHT AT THE BOTTOM'.

And so it was in the 1960s and 1970s. Before the boss came on his weekly perambulation around the ward with his registrar, housemen, and ward sister in obedient procession, the patients were all confined to bed, fags were put out, and some of the junior staff would have taken a beta-blocker if such were readily available. I think I was the first person in Brighton to prescribe beta-blockers – but for a patient, not a colleague.

It is probably difficult to comprehend, in those far-off days, just how much was done by juniors and how little day-to-day involvement many consultants had: I'm not saying, please note, that they spent all their time in their private consulting rooms or on the golf course, but many would have beds and out-patient clinics in several hospitals and spent hours travelling around the countryside. They would also undertake domiciliary visits at the request of a GP.[2] Nevertheless, we had to telephone the boss if a patient dared to die under our tender, loving care.

So we, as house physicians, were on the first rung of the ladder towards the deified status of the consultant, who was always addressed, of course, as 'sir'. There were few female consultants. Nevertheless, we had to contend with another formidable and almost entirely female-dominated hierarchy, the nursing staff.

The nursing staff

I think I learnt more about medicine from Sister E2 than from any doctor: she not only 'knew her stuff' but also was able to guide us through the foibles of the various consultants. 'Dr W will slaughter you if you call in a surgeon', 'Dr X won't speak to Dr Y', and 'Dr Z doesn't allow his patients to have such and such a drug (but Drs W, X, and Y do)'.

The nursing was of a very high standard: coming from St. Thomas Hospital and its Nightingale nurses, I think I was in a good position to comment! There was tight discipline, the nurses wore smart uniforms, and the wards were spotless. Most of the work was done by student nurses (only a sister and one or two trained nurses per ward), but one student distinguished herself by cleaning three patients' dentures

---

[2] It was some weeks before I realised that 'DV' in a GP's letter meant 'domiciliary visit', in contrast to the 'D & V' (diarrhoea and vomiting) of a toxic curry or tummy bug.

together in the same bowl of disinfectant… Most of the girls lived in the Nurses' Home on site, which came very handy for our frequent mess parties.

A high standard in any institution comes from leadership. The Matron was a formidable lady who wore a uniform: none of this 'Director of Nursing' in 'civvies' nonsense and multiplication of 'matrons for this and that!'. Interestingly, many of the smaller hospitals were run by a triumvirate of the Physician Superintendent (a senior consultant), the Matron, and the Hospital Secretary, who was very much an *administrator* rather than a *manager*. Neither the medical hierarchy nor the nursing hierarchy of those days would have submitted to being managed by a non-medical person. How things have changed – and not, to my mind, for the better…

One morning our ward clerk had made me a coffee after the ward round and was bringing it to the office when our lordly Matron swept by uttering just three words 'Tray, Mrs Thomas'. Even ward clerks came under the eagle eye of Matron!

But it was not all plain sailing: one morning, I came onto the ward to find a patient surrounded by a substantial amount of blood which was emanating from an elbow vein. Our kindly night sister decided that she would spare the patient the several blood tests required in a glucose tolerance test for diabetes (no finger-prick tests then) by inserting a Gordh needle[3] into a vein. I don't think she appreciated that Gordh needles were for putting fluids into people rather than taking them out. A visit to certain senior people was indicated (initiative here: no point in asking the boss), and that night sister was never seen again.

I'm not sure what the current procedure is in respect of administering controlled drugs, but in the1960s, a dose had to be checked not only by the nurse responsible for giving the injection but also by another suitably qualified member of staff and so I duly obliged our staff nurse by checking a dose of a DDA (Dangerous Drugs Act) before she jabbed it into the patient. A few days later, I was accosted in the middle of ward E2 by an irate assistant matron. 'Did you know that housemen are not permitted to check DDAs'? I replied, 'And did you know that assistant matrons are not legally permitted to prescribe them? I am.' MacMillan 1, assistant matron 0.

At the end of visiting time, it was customary for the ward sister to dismiss the visitors by ringing a large brass handbell: I think the lady concerned must have irritated me that day, so I got my own back by removing the clapper from the bell. It really was fun being a houseman… Even so, my boss's leaving testimonial noted that my relations with the nursing staff were always most cordial.

---

[3] A Gordh needle was a cannula inserted into vein to avoid multiple attacks from a needle and syringe when repeated blood tests were required.

The work

We filled in the forms; we took all the blood tests, we did the electrocardiograms using a very primitive and temperamental machine, we performed the lumbar punctures, and we did the male urinary catheterisations (at least I did: my female colleague was spared!), we hand-wrote the discharge summaries as well as attending the boss's weekly (yes, weekly) ward rounds – and still had time for fun.[4] Long hours and disturbed nights may have made us tired (even if we were only in our early twenties), but, above all, the little community in K Block enjoyed their work with little moaning, and we supported each other if things had gone badly. Contrast today, with short, fixed hours, 1 in 5 rotas, dissatisfied juniors, and most juniors living their own homes off-site: I suppose we had too much responsibility for our experience, but we just got on with it as that was a medical career was about.

Acute medicine in 1966

If we were unable to gain venous access from upper limb veins, we would perform a 'cut down' on an ankle vein and insert a Hamilton Bailey cannula, a metal device for administering fluids into a vein. As a budding surgeon, any excuse to attack a patient with a knife was welcome. I once

---

[4] A story is told relating to a London hospital: a new patient was admitted, and the incumbent of the next bed said to him 'The young bloke in the white coat is your doctor: the old buffer who comes with him once a week is on a refresher course'.

found what I took to be a juicy ankle vein, but on opening it, I found it was a solid tendon. The next morning I watched with concern as the patient took to his feet and I was much relieved when he did not fall over with a weak ankle!

Medical treatments were less exciting than operations: severe asthma attacks were sometimes treated by sedation with intramuscular paraldehyde (ouch!) and subcutaneous adrenaline 'one minim a minute'. Guess-work really. Diabetics were tricky, as blood sugar tests had to be sent to another hospital by taxi – the main hospital in the town and also the location of the town's only defibrillator. Handy in a cardiac arrest – and, by the way, some heart attack patients were on bedrest for four weeks, but I never saw a deep vein thrombosis resulting from this practice, and only a few patients received 'blood thinning' drugs. To mitigate the boredom for the patients, there were designated smoking hours on each ward and an ashtray on each bed table: in contrast to today, when smoking is regarded as a grievous sin, we assumed that everyone smoked; such was the culture of the late 1960s. It was not 'do you smoke?' but 'how many do you smoke?'

The real nightmare was haematemesis (vomiting blood) which seemed particularly common, I thought, in Brighton. I never saw a case at Thomas's, but that is probably because I was either coxing an VIII, practising music, or having a beer at King's College Faculty of Theology. I sussed out the cause of Brighton haematemesis: people on holiday were indulging their fancy for alcohol, exacerbated by the subsequent ingestion of *Alka Seltzer* which at that time contained aspirin, a potent cause of acute stomach ulcers. We had no endoscopes for diagnosis and treatment, which led to the occasional emergency removal of part of the stomach in the middle of the night. No modern anti-ulcer drugs either!

Some memorable cases

One evening we had a call from a GP who requested a bed for an octogenarian whose asthma attack had continued for a fortnight but, he added, she had never had asthma before. This did not add up, to say the least of it. A rather breathless lady appeared, with very noisy breathing. A quick examination revealed that the cause of her problem was not asthma but a hard mass in her neck (almost certainly a thyroid cancer) which was compressing her windpipe. The duty consultant surgeon, although accustomed to thyroid surgery, decided that an ENT surgeon should be called in to perform a tracheostomy. We all went off to theatre (exciting for a budding surgeon – more fun than dishing out pills), and by the early hours of the morning, the ENT surgeon put on his coat, turned to me, and said, 'MacMillan, change the tracheostomy tube in one week' and left the building. I should add that there was no ENT service in Brighton General.

This experienced surgeon, however, gave me one piece of advice which I have never forgotten and which has baled me out of a number of tricky problems: 'If you are called to a tracheostomy emergency, always take a Chevalier Jackson size 28 tube'. A good old-fashioned long silver tube with an introducer – much easier to insert into almost any trachy than the modern fancy cuffed plastic tubes!

I think this episode was seminal in turning my mind to ENT rather than gynae: I was up for a bit one night, but the gynae people seemed to be up all night every night…

On an idyllic late summer evening, I was asked to admit a very breathless lady who had been discharged only ten days before having been in heart failure: it was assumed that she had relapsed. However, I noticed a bruise on her left chest wall, which was very tender (that didn't fit), and apparently, she had slipped and hit her chest on the gas meter. There was no sign of heart failure, but a good old-fashioned clinical examination with a stethoscope revealed a pneumothorax (collapsed lung) and a deviated trachea. Diagnosis: tension pneumothorax following rib fracture. There was no time to mess about trying to get a chest X-ray, so I took a large needle and shoved it straight into her chest. With the resultant hiss of air, her symptoms were much improved, so I put in a proper chest drain and retired to bed. Would an unsupervised FY1 nowadays have the confidence to do what I was doing three months into my first job???

Many people will have memories of the summer of 1996, the year in which England won a football match – the World Cup, no less. My memories of this apparently seminal event in English history are largely confined to managing (or attempting to manage) a very severe diabetic crisis in a middle-aged woman. Her blood sugar was through the ceiling, she had classical diabetic ketoacidosis, and her potassium went up and down like a yoyo as I struggled with insulin dosage and fluid replacement: remember that the path lab was a taxi ride away, so no instant results. It was only when the nurses looked at her nether regions whilst passing a catheter that we discovered that the cause of her diabetic crisis was a large, fluctuant abscess. Fortunately, by midnight the biochemistry was (just about) under control and the boss popped in on his way home from a function (wearing his dinner jacket!) to check on progress. On Monday morning, he took me to one side: naturally expecting some caustic comments, I was amazed to hear him say that he was glad I was on call that day because, had it been any of the others, he thought we would have been facing a coroner's inquest. I will not forget World Cup Day.

Dermatology

In addition to the general medical work, I had to care for a few beds under the aegis of the consultant dermatologist (skin specialist). Dermatology was a complete mystery, with odd prescriptions such as Lassar's Paste and Dithranol in coal tar paste (still both available according to Google!), although the advent of topical steroids had transformed the speciality. I was astonished one evening when the boss rang and asked me to admit a dermatological emergency. I was somewhat disbelieving that there was such a thing as a dermatological emergency, but the poor patient had a rare and potentially fatal condition called toxic epidermal necrolysis due to a drug reaction (I think it may have been to phenobarbitone, but half a century on it's difficult to be sure). Fortunately, he recovered.

And finally

One story remains to be told, for the case of Mrs A marked a seminal point in my career: a moment which I shall never forget and which transformed me from being a student interested in medicine to a doctor who began to see (however inadequately) beyond the conventions, the drugs, and the operations to realise that our work is fundamentally about dealing with sick or dying people.

This good lady was dying from widespread lung cancer and, as was the custom in those days, was not told anything about her condition (*quel horreur!*). It was deemed appropriate by the boss that she should be moved to a nursing home for her last days, and I was instructed to make the necessary arrangements 'Don't tell her the diagnosis, of course, MacMillan, but have a word with her husband' quoth he who must be obeyed. Mr A went to see her and told his wife that she was about to die and would be transferred to a nursing home. After visiting hours, I was called to the ward to deal with a very distressed lady. How do you handle this when you have been a doctor for all of three months???

The only thought (and in retrospect, still a good decision) was to give her a dose of morphine and sort it out in the morning (remember that the name 'morphine' is derived from the Greek god of dreams 'Morpheus'). I went to see her before the ward round. 'Why did you not tell me? I knew all along'. There was only one answer 'because I was not allowed to'. Mrs A received Holy Communion and died in peace the next day. This brief episode, now 55 years ago, still brings tears to my eyes.

Farewell to Brighton

My all-too-short stint in the glorious summer of 1966 on the hill above Brighton discovering doctoring, watching the shipping in the Channel, and gazing over the twinkling lights of the town on a summer evening remains to this day the most enjoyable months of my career.

But it was time to move on, time to get on with being an ENT surgeon – albeit after a brief sojourn in the wilderness!

Chapter 2

Into the wilderness 1

Five locums

With my medical job under my belt, I was in a position to look seriously at planning a career in surgery: I have already noted that my initial intention was to become an obstetrician and gynaecologist, a speciality which I enjoyed as a student. We delivered babies; we sewed up the mothers after the traumatic arrival of their infant into the world (what their sex life was like after our efforts, I dread to think), and, in the 60s, there was still art in obstetric practice. If things are not 100% now, it's a Caesar, and that's that: no forceps to the after-coming head, no Kielland's forceps rotations or internal cephalic version, and so on. It was clear to me that the hours and chaos of obstetric practice might interfere with music and a civilised existence outside work, but a new hazard was looming on the horizon in the form of David Steel's Abortion Act of 1967. I have always been firmly opposed to the concept of termination of pregnancy unless there are overriding medical issues: I have never seen abortion as a justifiable moral act if performed purely for social reasons, even if veiled under various social circumstances.[5] To terminate a pregnancy in a sober teenage girl who has been raped is one thing; to terminate a pregnancy because another child would be inconvenient is

---

[5] I should add here that I am a deacon in the Church of England.

another. Although the Act did contain ‘conscientious objection clauses’, I could foresee that such a stance may not be ideal when applying for registrar posts in certain units, and so I turned to my second choice, ENT.

Unlike today, ENT was not a popular speciality in the late 1960s, but I was intrigued as a student to watch delicate middle ear surgery performed under the operating microscope. ENT appeared to be an exercise in precision surgery, often performed by a seated surgeon and with relatively little to keep one out of bed at night.

So the die was cast: I would swap Ds & Cs for Ts & As.[6]

Nil illegitimi carborundum

This mock-Latin phrase (don’t let the bastards grind you down) had a deep meaning for me over the next few months. I made an appointment towards the end of my medical job to speak with the senior ENT surgeon at Thomas’s to express my interest in his speciality: I think he was surprised. ‘Good. Apply for the house job in January (it was then October) and fill the time doing locums’. This looked promising (more about the locums later), but when the appointments were announced, I found that the ENT job had gone to a noted rugby player who, as far as I knew, had no interest in ENT – but the 1st. XV lacked a full-back. I confess to having a quiet chuckle when Thomas’s lost the first game in the hospitals’ rugby cup… I learnt from that experience to plough my own

[6] Dilatation and curettage: tonsils and adenoids.

furrow and never to rely on putative job offers: if you don't look after your career yourself, nobody is going to do it for you!

Five locum jobs in four months

This phase of my career was unsettling: I had exemplary references from Brighton ('one of the best young men we have had here recently'), but a pre-registration job in surgery was becoming elusive. It's all planned out today by the medical schools, but for me, it was a frantic look at the adverts in the *British Medical Journal* each Friday, and I attended eight job interviews before I was offered what turned out to be an exceptional posting in a very ordinary hospital in London's East End.

The first stop was a two-week locum in general surgery at a little hospital in Bromley. A pleasant place, with good colleagues but, again, no bleeps. Coloured lights this time. I do remember having to cover Casualty from time to time: a typical Saturday brought domestic and shopping accidents in the morning, muddy people with sports injuries in the afternoon, and the inevitable drunks in the evening (and night). The only other memory of my two weeks at Bromley was of a senior surgeon advising us that London tap water was sufficiently sterile to be used for irrigation of the bladder after prostate operations. Eeek!

I then found myself spending six weeks at the Kent and Sussex Hospital in Tunbridge Wells, the only job I have not enjoyed throughout my career. It was a humourless mess, the work not exactly stimulating, and the food was awful. One supper time, I marched into the kitchen and demanded to be allowed to cook my own supper, and I'm sure I dined better on my vegetarian omelette than the other doctors did that evening. I fell out with the boss over the question of chaperoning: I announced that I could not perform comprehensive examinations on his female patients because the nursing staff would not provide chaperones. 'Can't you trust yourself, MacMillan?' 'Of course, sir, but a chaperone is a necessary courtesy towards a female patient'.

I left Tunbridge Wells with an immense sense of relief and ended up back in London at St. James's Hospital, Balham.

'Jimmy's' was an old workhouse-type hospital within walking distance of my home and the site of an exceptional gastric surgical unit within what was, essentially, an ordinary district general hospital (DGH). I was to be a gynaecology house surgeon (no obstetrics) for two weeks with the usual 1 in 2 rota and a tiny on-call room that was perhaps two feet wider than the very narrow bed. I enjoyed this job, but it struck me that pregnancy was a rather risky affair as we had a long procession of miscarriages and ectopic pregnancies – plus a few DIY abortions. In 1967 the contraceptive pill was not as ubiquitous as in later years, and there was no 'morning after' pill. I also wondered, if pregnancy and childbirth are purely natural events (as we are told), why we should need an entire army of doctors, midwives, and nurses to look after its potential alarums and excursions! But I digress; one day, I had to attend an interview, so I turned up to work in a three-piece suit with a stiff white collar (*de rigueur*) and performed a D & C or two before going off to attend the interview. I thought (perhaps wickedly) of the similarly attired consultants who graced the NHS with their presence to do a couple of cases before going off to more lucrative employment in London W1 and leaving it to the registrar to finish the list…

Did I want to return to my initial career choice – no!

Anything to pay the bills! I applied for a locum in geriatrics at the Whittington Hospital (yes, called after Dick Whittington and built near the site where he turned back to London with his cat to become Lord Mayor), but the post had already been filled: I was offered a couple of weeks in Casualty instead. I jumped at the chance: action! However, I was pre-registration (FY1), and the powers that be deemed that, with my lowly status, I could not be left alone to run Casualty at weekends. After a few days, they changed their minds, and I discovered what it was like 'to be alone in Casualty on a dark night', as one of my anatomy lecturers put it. Nevertheless, I thrived on this, and I have one remarkable memory of the Whittington on Sunday evenings: many of the juniors were resident, and at that time, we had number of colleagues from the Indian sub-continent. The

Indian doctors made a curry, and the Brits provided the beer. Who needs 'diversity training'…?

The final stop on this perambulation would be Queen Mary's Sidcup, now a gleaming modern hospital, but in 1967 the patients were housed in wooden huts, whilst the doctors lived in a Georgian (or Georgian-style) mansion. As a locum, I was billeted in the nursing sisters' quarters, and a nocturnal visit to the wards took me on a footpath through a field of cows. The job was routine general surgery, but I recall one emergency admission of a man who had complained of sudden, severe abdominal pain: clinically, he had a small bowel obstruction, so we proceeded to open him up (no CTs and no laparoscopy in 1967), carried out through what was called 'the resident surgeon's incision' – a right paramedian. His bowel was obstructed by a mass of peanuts stuck behind an obstruction which was due to a very rare congenital peritoneal adhesion. The adhesion was divided, and the peanuts sent on their way to the colon.[7] Note that there was no consultant presence!

At Sidcup, I received news that I had been appointed House Surgeon to Mile End Hospital in the East End of London. Mile End was a very ordinary district hospital in a run-down area, but at least it was a permanent job – and an ENT consultant from St. Bartholomew's Hospital came once a week. I'm not sure to this day whether it was luck, the

---

[7] Douglas MacMillan, 'An unusual case of intestinal obstruction', *British Journal of Clinical Practice*, (1969).

prayers of St. Blaise (patron saint of the throat), or the household gods, *Lares et Penates*, that led to the beginning (at last!) of my career in ENT.

Chapter 3

House Surgeon

(FY1 part 2)

Mile End Hospital

I arrived at Mile End Hospital in the East End of London on a grey, drizzly, cold afternoon in March 1967, relieved at last to have a six-month appointment where I could begin my surgical career. Like Brighton, the hospital was a Victorian building with a few 'add-ons', notably new operating theatres, which were opened while I was there: in these days of centralisation of healthcare, it is perhaps difficult to conceive of the East End being littered with small hospitals – Mile End itself, Bethnal Green, St. Leonard's at Haggerston, the London Jewish Hospital, the Mildmay Mission Hospital, and others. Many GPs worked in single-handed practices, and the 'big hospital' was The London (now The Royal London) in Whitechapel, which eventually swallowed up Mile End. It is fair to say that the East End was a rather deprived area with some regions of dubious morality and was perhaps not the safest place to walk at night. For a social picture of the area, I can best point you to the BBC's *Call the Midwife* series (2012 –): although showing life in Poplar from the late 1950s to the early 60s, there are many social factors with which I can identify from my time at Mile End a few years later. Essentially a working-class area, the population comprised cockneys (bless their hearts!), other East Enders, and a large Jewish population, but very few immigrants from other countries, a pattern that would change in the later 1970s and 1980s.

Mile End was typical of the small hospitals of its day: two or three consultant general physicians, two or three consultant general surgeons, some obstetricians and paediatricians (the East End was a very fecund area), and anaesthetists who seemed to me like peripatetic givers of gas, going from hospital to hospital giving anaesthetics but with no apparent 'fixed abode'. The consultant staff was supported by the usual batch of housemen and registrars, but, to this day, I do not know whether these 'training' posts were inspected and/or approved! There was a tiny casualty department: indeed, the local populace spoke of going to casualty as 'going up the Bancroft', for the hospital address was 'Bancroft Road'. The hospital employed one (yes, one) casualty officer of SHO status, so the surgical housemen took turns on casualty duty. It was fun in the East End on Saturday nights… and a very formative experience! Talking of *Call the Midwife* reminds me that the first person I saw at Mile End apart from the gate porter was a nun-midwife wearing the delightful blue habit of a Sister of the Anglican Community of St. John the Divine, translated by the BBC into Nonnatus House. Classicists, please consider the name of the house!

The Mess

It is perhaps difficult for junior doctors to conceive – in these days of 1 in 5 rotas – how different life was if one worked the normative 1 in 2. Most people lived in the hospital as opposed to just staying overnight when on call, and we had a specific doctors' mess where we ate, slept, and socialised: a place where we could openly rejoice in our triumphs, receive support when things were hard, and enjoy a degree of exclusiveness as we began our careers in a learned profession. I am as much of an egalitarian as the next man, but nevertheless, it was good to sit down with a coffee and the newspaper after lunch in a quiet mess common room and chat (or not) with fellow juniors and seniors alike. I still remember my boss struggling with *The Times* crossword with junior doctors perched on each side of his armchair!

I forgot to mention this when writing about Brighton, but we housemen (or women, although they were still entitled house*men*) received free board and lodging. Unfortunately, it occurred to some bureaucrats that doctors had to eat whether on or off on duty, so the privilege of free meals was abolished during my time at Mile End. Fortunately, however, the clumsy NHS administration had failed to establish a system for collecting the cash at mealtimes for several months: the food wasn't bad, either, especially considering that it was, to all intents and purposes, still free…

Having residential quarters in the middle of the hospital, the journey to the wards in the wee small hours was easy, unlike the perambulation at Brighton. I recall being woken one night by the duty night sister who requested my presence on the ward. The voice sounded familiar, and in my somnolent state, I wondered whether I should go to E2 or E3: the night sister from Brighton had also migrated to east London! Another memory of getting up in the night was walking across the hospital garden to Casualty and smelling Charrington's brewery in action. No beer when on call nowadays.

Before we go to the theatre (the whole purpose of being a surgeon), I would remind my readers that we had far fewer diagnostic aids: ultrasound was in its early days and belonged to obstetricians, and of course, there were no CT or MRI scans. We were trained in the arts of history, taking and making a physical examination before plunging into investigations: writing in 2021 during Covid. I wonder how one does this in a telephone consultation…

In the theatre

But what of the surgery? In those days, 'general surgeons' were *general* surgeons at home doing thyroids, mastectomies, and prostatectomies, as well as all the routine and emergency abdominal surgery. It was at Mile End that I witnessed my one and only Harris suprapubic prostatectomy (thank God!). We had no thoracic or vascular facilities but made a good trade in high saphenous ligation and stripping of varicose veins: I don't think the aetiology of 'VVs' was really understood, so it really was a basic plumbing job – one to which I was personally subjected some years in the future. My boss also undertook orthopaedic surgery but without any of the sophistication of modern technology. On one occasion, we found that the Küntscher nail which he had inserted into a femoral shaft fracture was not only too long but also irremovable. Undeterred, the boss sent for a hacksaw, had it 'boiled up' (sterilised!), and shortened the offending nail. I understood that he was an accomplished handyman in his home life…

The first real joy of my stay at Mile End was the opportunity to put on a gown and gloves and operate, usually under the close supervision of my Turkish registrar, who sadly died well before his time only a few years later. The incision and drainage of all sorts and conditions of abscesses were usually entrusted to me, and it is, I think, one of the most rewarding procedures in surgery. An incision, a liberal discharge of pus, and the secure knowledge that the patient will feel much better very quickly. Nowadays, to my mind, there is too much faffing about aspirating abscesses with needles: put a knife in, let out the evil humours, drain the wound, and all will be well! Under supervision, I operated on piles, repaired hernias (no laparoscopes, of course), and attacked varicose veins – one leg for me, one for the registrar – but the real delight was appendicectomies, of which I did about ten and usually took about half an hour each. One of these took place on an August evening during the Proms season, and we had the radio on, listening to Beethoven's *Eroica* symphony while we operated. The last movement has quite a long coda (with which I, as a musician, was very familiar), so I slowed down my closure of the wound so that I could tie the final stitch exactly on the concluding chord of the symphony.

I doubt if any FY1 – or probably even an FY2 – in the present day could match this wealth of operative experience. They are too tied up with ward work: so was I, but I was expected to be present in theatre for the boss's list, so I got up early or stayed late (no European Working Time Directive) to do my ward work and take the bloods. How do we recruit people into surgery if they do not see the cutting edge (excuse the pun) of the speciality? It may be either because I am getting old or because I am viewing the past through rose-tinted glasses, but when I read that young doctors are not going into surgery 'because it would upset their work/life balance', I am concerned. As a young surgeon, my work/life balance was 'operate, operate, operate', and anything else had to be fitted in. A saying from the days of the Royal Flying Corps in 1913 reads, 'Time in the air alone will make a good pilot': could we not say the same about time in theatre and surgeons?

Casualty

I have already mentioned Casualty: this was very different from the present-day consultant-led high-tech environment and was staffed by very junior doctors who were largely left to fend for themselves. Cut fingers, minor fractures (I learnt to manipulate Colles wrist fractures while a house surgeon), abscesses, and inevitably, drunks were the life-blood of our stints in 'Cas'. Indeed, I think the one thing that has not changed radically in all my years in medicine is Casualty/A&E at midnight on Saturdays… It was at Mile End that I first was called upon to 'section' a psychiatric patient who was brandishing a carving knife with the intention of attacking his mother-in-law: most men do not get as far as finding the carving knife. Very early one Sunday morning (i.e., well before breakfast), a very young man presented himself with a headache: he confessed to having consumed about ten pints of beer. There was no sign of head injury or meningitis, so after a quick 'what do you expect' I threw him out and went back to bed.

ENT

Although my job was primarily about general surgery, on Thursday afternoons, I became the ENT houseman. A consultant from St. Bartholomew's Hospital came weekly to do a small out-patient clinic, followed by a list of short procedures; inevitably, most of these were tonsils and adenoids (Ts & As) – fantastic house surgeon fodder. In outpatients, I learnt the old art of cleaning the ear with cotton wool mounted on a Jobson Horne probe (no microscopes or microsuction) and rapidly discovered that the way to placate East End mothers was to put their snotty offspring on the list for the removal of its tonsils and adenoids. I could wax lyrical on this fabulous operation if it is performed for the correct reasons, and please be warned that I may well do so before this book is finished! After the clinic, we proceeded to the theatre, where I was taught how to perform the surgery, and after a few training sessions was left to get on with the list while the boss attended to his administrative duties. Present-day trainees will be astonished to learn that I did 45 Ts & As in my six-month placement: none had to be returned to the theatre for control of bleeding, either![8] I also made it my business to learn to deal with nosebleeds, from packing the nose to cauterising bleeding vessels with an electro-cautery: amazing what one can learn from a textbook! I am reminded of the old surgical adage 'see one, do one, teach one'… I let it be known that I was interested in ENT, and one of the consultant physicians whose patient I had reviewed assumed that I was the ENT registrar. His patient had the only Pott's Puffy Tumour that I have ever seen, but this was a job for the boss, who introduced me to trephining and draining the frontal sinus. At the end of my

---

[8] As a senior surgeon, my primary haemorrhage rate was below 1%.

time at Mile End, an operating microscope arrived in the theatre – and so did grommets.

Goodbye, obstetrics and gynaecology!

People

It is always difficult to classify everything, but I would like to make a few disconnected comments which remain fond memories of the summer of 1967. On a Saturday evening, the medical houseman and surgical registrar would often nip down to the pub (three minutes away, but I can't exactly recall its name now, although I think it was The Half Moon) for quick a half-pint, followed on their return by the surgical houseman and the medical registrar – and I do not recall even having to pay for the beer. If we were needed, the switchboard operator just 'phoned the pub: no mobiles!

And there was Harold. Harold was a fifty-odd-year-old man with Down's Syndrome (it was rare for Down's patients to survive to 50 in those days) who was on our ward for weeks, with apparently little wrong: I suppose it's what we would now classify as 'bed blocking'. Anyway, Harold was a real jewel with a heart of gold who got to know all the patients: he served their morning tea and their late evening drink with joy and friendliness that I hope many will remember.

I grew to love and respect the East Enders: lovely, generous people who would do anything for you if you treated them as your equals, which indeed they are. It is interesting to reflect that I received more gifts from patients in six months in the deprived East End of London than in six years in leafy Surrey with its plethora of 4x4 automobiles…

Chapter 4

Casualty Officer

St. Mary's Hospital, Paddington

Before I go any further, I should explain that what is now called A & E or Emergency Department was known from time immemorial until the 1970s as Casualty or 'Cas' for short. Inevitably many of the attendees were not casualties in the strict sense, but it was a relatively easy way to get to see a doctor: it strikes me that little has changed in this respect over the years with the decline in the availability of GP appointments. A 'Cas job' was a requirement for trainee surgeons wishing to take the general FRCS examination, although surgeons who were specialising in ophthalmology or ENT were exempt from this as we had specialty-specific fellowships: nevertheless, it seemed a good idea to spend six months being frightened out of my wits in Casualty at St. Mary's, Paddington.[9] Now the real challenge of the FRCS was not the final examination but the primary, a very rigorous examination in anatomy, physiology, and pathology with an enormous failure rate. Since Mary's was a teaching hospital, there was the added advantage of the presence of an anatomy department for teaching the medical students, and I managed to get access to the department as an unpaid demonstrator – I hasten to add that this was not an

---

[9] Unlike today, the diploma was simply 'FRCS' without any specialty qualifier.

act of benevolence on my part, but a useful adjunct to Last's *Anatomy: Regional and Applied* and it really helped in studying anatomy to see it 'for real' in the dissected cadaver.

The Casualty Department was, by teaching hospital standards, tiny but nevertheless presided over by a formidable Welsh sister. There were three surgical casualty officers and also medical casualty officers – an excellent arrangement as we surgeons were not bothered by drug overdoses, chest pain, and shortage of breath and could get on with sewing up wounds, manipulating fractures, and draining abscesses. Twice a day, a very junior anaesthetist (eeek!) would attend to give short general anaesthetics. We worked a 1 in 3 rota, the weekends being something of a trial: one ran the department single-handed from Saturday morning until Monday morning and then attended the fracture clinic. Not much energy left for the afternoon anatomy demonstrating!

One of my colleagues had trained with me at medical school, and we were initially in the same year, but he overtook me by six months as I failed surgery finals the first time round. He did three jobs at the teaching hospital whilst I was labouring in the medical bush.[10] Interestingly, I had a much more varied experience and a much greater degree of independence in my practice than my teaching hospital-trained contemporary. Three teaching hospital jobs looks

---

[10] Not, please, 'the sticks': in classical mythology, the River Styx formed the boundary between earth and the underworld.

good on the CV, but I'm glad that I worked in very ordinary hospitals – perhaps because I am said to be a bit 'Bohemian, rebellious, and free-spirited'!

Trying to convey the flavour of working as a non-resident in a department when there was little opportunity to integrate socially into the hospital environment will be difficult: I turned up for work on time (underground permitting!), secluded myself in Cas and then went home if I were not on duty for the evening and night. The shift system had yet to be invented: one worked all day, and if one happened to be the duty doctor, all evening and all night as well – followed again by the fracture clinic, itself a mixture of instruction and admonishment. Unlike Brighton and Mile End, my 'mess life' was confined to lunches and dinners: fortunately, someone had discovered an ancient statute in the hospital archives that decreed that doctors should be provided with a beer at mealtimes… I had a ghastly on-call room just above the ambulance entrance: the ambulance sirens usually preceded a telephone summons, and if it seemed that nothing much would be required, I went to Casualty in a white coat over my dressing gown and pyjamas – but always wearing a silk cravat.

Work-wise, I let it be known that I wanted to be an ENT surgeon, so all ENT casualties were channelled in my direction, and I also arranged with the ENT out-patient sister to use the facilities of her department for cauterising bleeding noses. I don't think the consultants were told.

Incidentally, there was no such thing as a consultant in Casualty, but the department was benignly overlooked (on rare occasions) by an orthopaedic consultant. I was able to advance my operative skills in a weekly 'lumps and bumps' minor ops list.

As I have said, the personal contacts were too ephemeral for me to write much about the people I worked with and treated, so I will treat you to a few cases reports to give a flavour of what was actually a rather enjoyable job. Most of the patients presented with the usual mixture of minor injuries, pain, and infections: the really serious stuff went to Paddington General up the road.

Where to start? There is no logical order in which to present my cases, so I should begin at the place where any medical consultation begins 'What seems to be wrong?' On one occasion, a party of four were visiting London from the north of England and, being unaccustomed to escalators on the tube, had cascaded down the last few steps, landing in a rather undignified heap. They had the expected mixture of minor cuts and bruises and were duly sent on their way after treatment. I was, however, nonplussed by the fourth patient: after I asked him which part of himself he had injured, he answered that he wasn't hurt but had just come in to be checked over. This seemingly silly episode focused my mind on the opening gambit: one could not really begin a consultation without some sort of overture to indicate the nature of the patient's problem. The episode also gave me new respect for vets: cats can't tell you what's wrong, however loudly they miaow.

Inevitably, Casualty is a window into the less agreeable traits of humanity. One evening a reasonably sober man appeared, bleeding from a nasty knife wound. It was easy enough to fix, but I was glad that I would not be on duty the next evening for (in a strong South Welsh accent) he quoth, 'I'm going home to get my bloody hatchet and do that bloke'. Alcohol, of course, features large in many events in Casualty: many of those intoxicated patients have massive social problems and may be homeless, but, despite the chaos they can cause, it is impossible to be angry with them for the bottle may be the only way they can try to escape from their untold misery. A few drinks, a few stitches in a scalp wound, and being taken to the cells in a Police van is a miserable fate for a man (rarely a woman), and I do not see how any do-gooding social worker or psychologist (or, indeed, a politician) can solve this problem. After all, society has lived with it for thousands of years. Treating the sometimes-violent drunks (I was never physically assaulted) is just part of the casualty doctor's job and not a pleasant part at that: it was not uncommon to find, amongst the matted blood-stained hair, stitches that had been inserted into a previous wound but never removed.

I found myself on duty on Bonfire Night, an experience to put one off fireworks for life, unless, that is, they are in a formal display run by a pyrotechnician. Fireworks going off in a man's trouser pocket could be threatening to his reproductive capacity, minor burns, and, worse still, eye injuries, all turned up on 5 November. During a lull in proceedings, I was sitting quietly in my room trying to learn some anatomy when a noisy gaggle of teenagers appeared. One was pushed to fore, clutching his ear, ''is ear's been shot off by a rocket, doc'. This, I thought, demands action. I did not want the department cluttered up with a crowd of hysterical teenagers, so I turned to the assembled company. 'You lot go off and look for his ear, and I'll see to him'. Off they went. Removing the dressing, I found that there was indeed a piece of ear missing, but the neat semi-circular chunk missing from the border of the ear looked more like a bite than a missile injury. Anyway, I indulged in some rather fancy wound closing, and I hope he had a reasonable (if slightly smaller) ear. As a budding ENT surgeon, it was fun to do this surgery: it was certainly not the last time in my career, but it was the only time when the cause of the injury was a rocket attack…

But then, life in Casualty is not just about drunks and ruffians who get into fights: most of our attendees had minor injuries incurred domestically or in the street or on Saturdays on the football field. 99% of the patients were perfectly decent people who had just met with one of life's accidents. The medical students did most of the simple suturing (no tissue glues in 1967), whereas we Casualty Officers did the more exciting procedures, like whipping off bits of a finger

- and toe-nails to drain abscesses, manipulating Colles' fractures, and slapping on plaster casts – messy but great fun and one could try to be something of a sculptor!

I have mentioned 'drunks and ruffians', but Casualty really was a window on the world, a place when even in one's twenties, one really met the seamier side of life (thank goodness gynaecological disasters were not in our remit as surgical casualty officers). I was horrified late one evening when a well-dressed young woman waiting to see a doctor was forcibly abducted by her equally well-dressed and well-spoken man. Protesting, she was bundled into his waiting Jaguar. It was too late for police intervention. I have often wondered what became of her.

There is no doubt in my mind that every young doctor – whether they wish to be a surgeon, a physician, a psychiatrist, a GP, or whatever – should have a few months in what is now A & E. Not only will they see life 'but not as we know it', but they will have the stimulus of not knowing what will be the next case that walks in, staggers in, or is carried in by ambulance or policemen. The job can only broaden the medical mind, sharpen clinical judgment, and make the doctor stand very firmly on his or her own feet for probably the first time in their career. If they can't hack it, they should run away from clinical medicine: I would not want them to be my doctor!

I will gloss over the next four months of my career as a junior doctor, for they were occupied only with lectures, reading, reading, and more reading. I have already alluded to the pre-surgical *tour de force* called the Primary FRCS, and so I enrolled in the appropriate course at that august institution in Lincoln's Inn Fields, the Royal College of Surgeons. The daily timetable was simple to memorise: read for an hour, lectures all morning, lunch, read for an hour and a half, go home and read for four and a half hours. Perhaps because I took Sundays off, I failed the exam the first time round.

There is, however, an ENT-related memory. The anatomy lecturer gazed over his class and asked, 'What do we know about the tonsils and adenoids'? 'One, they exist: and, two, why do they exist – to buy cream Rolls Royces for Ear, Nose, and Throat surgeons'.[11] With his words ringing in my ears, I took the opportunity to visit my ENT boss from Mile End in his rooms in Harley Street to discuss my career and subsequently found myself appointed without an interview as House Surgeon to the ENT Department of the Royal and Ancient Hospital of St. Bartholomew.

---

[11] I never had one.

Chapter 5

ENT House Surgeon

St. Bartholomew's Hospital, London

On the bright, sunny Saturday morning that heralded 29 June 1968, I made my way through the Henry VIII gate for my first view of the serene eighteenth-century square of St. Bartholomew's Hospital, with its trees and bubbling fountain. I was almost alone apart from a couple of nurses and the hospital chaplain in his robes taking Holy Communion to the wards: I knew at once that I would be happy in this most ancient of British hospitals, and Bart's has been my 'medical spiritual home' since that June day so long ago.

I had started on a Saturday as a weekend locum because my predecessor had requested leave to go to a wedding: from my point of view, it was a good arrangement because, having a little previous ENT experience, I could easily get to grips with the job and a ward full of complex patients. Like junior commissioned officers, housemen were addressed as 'Mr' and, duly clad in my white coat; I found my way through a subterranean tunnel to the Queen Elizabeth Block and Henry Butlin ward for my first ward round with the duty Senior Registrar. I was struck by the sheer order and discipline, the friendliness, the elegant nurses' uniforms, and Barts' jargon – which took a while to comprehend. What, I thought in heaven's name, do they mean by 'a message for the Pink'?

Henry Butlin was a mixed ward, men and women each in their own four-bedded bays, and we also had a nine-bed children's unit, which saved us from paediatric interference. Patients remained in hospital for much longer than is customary nowadays, so there was far more social interaction: the women looked after the kids, and the men pushed the tea-trollies. Just a big ENT family!

Bart's ward sisters ran tight ships and could be imposing in their blue uniforms and tall white caps: on my first morning on the ward, I was summoned to Sister's sitting room for coffee, where I was introduced to her 'Pink', ranked as a junior sister, 'Pinks' being so-called because of their beautiful pink uniforms, again surmounted by a slightly shorter white cap.[12] The Pink and I became life-long friends.[13] But I digress: I spent most of the weekend reading the case notes and re-writing all the prescriptions, or, in Barts' terminology, re-writing the 'Blue Boards'. As the City of London was essentially non-residential, we had few emergency admissions, so I had a quiet weekend – at least by surgical standards.

On Monday, 1 July, I was prepared for the battle to commence!

---

[12] All uniform hemlines were required to be eleven inches from the ground, regardless of the height of the wearer.

[13] We discovered that we had a mutual connection in that her father had been a curate at the church in Pimlico which I attended and where I acted as sub-deacon: to quote a Psalm, 'we walked in the house of God as friends'.

The ENT Department

We were, by ENT standards of the time, a large department with four consultants, two senior registrars, a 'middle-grade' registrar (another Barts' term!), and two house surgeons – so back to one in two on call. In these days of considerable consultant presence, it is interesting to reflect how much was done in the past by the juniors: the consultants were often also on the staff at other hospitals, as well as having a private practice based in London W1… I suspect, however, that they knew more about what was going on than we thought, despite perhaps having only two or three clinics and one or two operating lists per week. In those days, all the consultants would now be called 'generalists': there was no separation into otology, rhinology, or head and neck surgery, and all were capable of doing mastoids, stapedectomies, nasal surgery, and laryngectomies although, to my recollection, only one of our consultants indulged in cosmetic rhinoplasty or 'nose jobs'. Sadly, ENT surgeons in those days usually left the thyroids to general surgeons.

We house surgeons did the usual dogsbody jobs, but nevertheless, we were expected to be present in theatre for the boss's lists. These started at 0830: breakfast was not served in the mess until 0800, so one had to do the routine ward work before breakfast: neither lateness nor absence was tolerated (quite rightly!). But how could a would-be surgeon miss theatre… we were given a good share of the Ts

& As and grommets, and I made my first forays into nasal septal surgery, polypectomy, and inferior meatal antrostomy (no fancy endoscopic nasal surgery in 1968). We could be extracted from theatre to deal with emergencies and, as a point of courtesy, to attend a consultant from another department who had been asked to review one of our patients: such a request was made on a 'yellow board'. Inevitably we made trips to Casualty, but there were few night calls. I suppose I would have been summoned from my bed about one in ten duty nights: the obstetric house surgeons had a rather different experience. Good decision, MacMillan!

We were usually allocated a small list of simple follow-up cases in the outpatient department and rapidly mastered the art of cleaning ears using the microscope, of which there were only two in the department – theatre and out-patients. All very low tech, but very good training in *clinical* medicine. All out-patient departments of whatever speciality will have their *bête noire* patients: one of our patients had suffered from a discharging ear for years. Although not a serious medical problem, it was a massive irritation to him, and he was thoroughly fed up and had that 'something must be done' look; he presented on a very regular basis requesting cleaning of his ear. One day he turned up with a broad smile: the doctor asked if his ear had stopped discharging: 'No', he said. 'my wife died last week'. We doctors do see the humanity in the raw.

There were, of course, no flexible endoscopes, so we learnt the art (for such it was) of indirect laryngoscopy and examination of the post-nasal space using a mirror. In these far-off days, all thyroidectomy patients were required to have a 'vocal cord check' to ensure that both vocal cords moved freely: if the patient subsequently developed a hoarse voice, a nagging judicial finger could be pointed at the surgeon. On my first Sunday evening (36 hours into my job), a general surgical house surgeon paged me to say that he had forgotten to ask for an ENT registrar cord check on Friday (yellow board again!), so he thought he would ask me in order to avert a ticking-off from his boss on Monday morning. I refused: if there was a problem post-operatively and the case came to court, I doubt if the judge would be impressed if I said I was only in the first 36 hours of my formal ENT training. One learns to cover one's back, even if an unknown colleague lands in the proverbial!

But to return to Henry Butlin ward: we had our own ward (like neurosurgery, thoracic surgery, and ophthalmology) and were free from medical cases being dumped in our beds. The day's business was decreed during the registrar's round, a three-line whip if you were not in the theatre, and we were always accompanied by a senior nurse, Sister herself, the Pink, or what was called a 'Belt'. Belts were girls (no men then!) in their fourth year of training for their Barts Hospital badge, so they were already State Registered Nurses (RGNs today). Some were employed on night duty to assist the dark queen known as Night Sister, and, as they were peripatetic, going from ward to ward, they gained the epithet 'Flash Belts'.

So much for generalities: it's time for some ENT! I think it is fair to say that I began my ENT career at the turning point between unchanging traditional practice and modern technological advances. The advent of the operating microscope had totally transformed otology and had enabled surgeons to perform stapedectomies and middle ear reconstructive surgery: the old days of mallet and gouge mastoidectomy performed with the naked eye had given way to delicate microsurgical procedures using the drill and newly-devised instruments, although some of the very senior surgeons still began mastoid surgery with a mallet and gouge before moving into the mid-twentieth century with microscope and drill! The really stunning ear operation was the removal of the otosclerotic fixed stapes[14] and its prosthetic replacement, enabling millions of suffers from otosclerosis to ditch their cumbersome hearing aids (as a colleague said, 'plug, wire, box' – behind the ear aids were still a couple of years away). And, of course, there was the humble grommet, used in the treatment of glue ear. This often-derided simple, safe and inexpensive operation enabled thousands of children to hear while they 'grew out of' glue ear, saving their education and social integration.

---

[14] The third of the chain of three small bones in the middle ear.

Nasal surgery really was the Cinderella, substantially unchanged since the 1930s: perhaps the less said, the better, except for one (to my mind, dangerous) curiosity, the cocaine sensitivity test. Cocaine was used in nasal surgery to reduce bleeding, and the patients had to undergo a 'cocaine sensitivity test' to make sure they were not allergic to the stuff. A small dose was injected, and the pulse was monitored for half an hour; a rapid heart rate suggested sensitivity to cocaine, although, in my humble opinion, anyone who was really cocaine sensitive would just have dropped dead!

Although the microscope had just come into use for the examination of the larynx, I could never enthuse about head and neck cancer surgery: many of the operations were long, fraught with complications, and often heralded a very poor prognosis. This particularly applied to the replacement of the oesophagus by a segment of the bowel. We talk much nowadays (and rightly) about detailed consent for operations, but it was hardly thus in the late 1960s. Patients were expected to take the surgeon's advice, never mind discussing complications and outcomes, but we tended to avoid too much medical jargon. I recall one lady consenting to a radical throat operation with bowel replacement which was described on the consent form as 'having my guts brought up to help me swallow', a note written by our ward clerk rather than a consultant surgeon! I think we have improved in our communication with our patients, but there is often much to be desired: I still return to the story of Mrs A at Brighton told in the first chapter of this book.

In my forty-five-year career in ENT, I only encountered three cases of 'crash tracheostomy', a tracheostomy performed in a great emergency in the patient's bed and under a nominal local anaesthetic, but it was, in all three cases, life-saving. Fortunately, I never had to do one myself. One Friday afternoon, we were quietly having a cup of tea towards the end of the clinic when we had a call from X-ray to say that a laryngeal cancer patient who had just arrived from another hospital was unable to breathe. Quick as a flash, the boss said, 'It's the knife', and we rushed to X-ray where the poor man had a crash trachy, undoubtedly saving his life. We took his larynx out later that evening. Very late bedtime.

And so to the tonsils and adenoids, the bread-and-butter operation associated with ENT surgeons, a brilliant training ground for housemen, a source of untold guineas in Harley Street, and an operation that really transformed children's lives – with the proviso that the latter only applied if it was done for the correct reasons. As a procedure to prevent recurrent tonsillitis, it is 100% effective: just point out to those opposed to it that if one has no tonsils, one cannot get tonsillitis… Very large tonsils and adenoids can cause difficulty eating and obstructed breathing at night, and, again, the operation is hugely successful. How often did I hear in the follow-up clinic 'he/she eats better, sleeps better, has more energy, and has caught up at school'? What it does *not* do is help the snotty, catarrhal child who does not have tonsillitis but just gets recurrent colds (me as a four-year-old!), and the reason for its ill-repute is because many surgeons in the generations before me (!) saw it as a panacea for all child health problems. I still think it is one of the best operations in the ENT armamentarium, and I don't care what paediatricians, psychiatrists, trendy Guardianistas, and similar do-gooders say!

To conclude this chapter – we shall return to Barts when 'I came back as a registrar'– I thought I should offer a little insight into the humour and humanity of this most ancient London hospital. At the door of each room in the junior doctors' residence was a small blackboard on which the occupant would leave a message for the maid as to whether early morning tea or coffee was required: should the girlfriend be imported for the night, the doctor simply requested two teas or coffees, with or without sugar. Opposite the hospital in Giltspur Street lay the White Hart pub (now closed): in front of a patient, we did not say 'see you in the White Hart at six' but 'meet you in the anaemia clinic at six'. Alcohol could be prescribed as a medication, and I well remember a consultant turning to me after he had removed a medical student's tonsils with the instruction 'Board him for a bottle of Guinness a day, MacMillan. He's the full-back in the 1st. XV'. Medical terminology was even applied to architectural features; a short tunnel leading to a ward block was universally known as 'the colostomy'…

I end on a historic and celebratory note. Since the sixteenth century, the second Wednesday in May has been designated 'View Day', a day when traditionally the hospital showed its work to the local community and was inspected by its governors. During my days at Barts, there was no clinical work on that Wednesday afternoon: the men wore smart suits (usually with a floral buttonhole), and the girls decked themselves in suitable finery. Ward sisters made a trip (in uniform) to the Old Covent Garden Flower Market to acquire flowers (often free, or at least at a reduced price!) to decorate their wards and subsequently presented a magnificent tea for their nurses and doctors. The governors, led by the Beadle in his gown and bearing his wand, visited selected wards and departments: although now a rather curtailed ceremonial exercise with just a church service and a reception, it remains one of the great traditions of this remarkable, unique, and historic hospital.

Floruit floret floreat

Chapter 6

Senior House Officer

The Royal National Throat, Nose, and Ear Hospital, Gray's Inn Road

During my six months stint at Barts, I passed my primary FRCS examination and was poised on the first rung of the surgical ladder. I was very much ready for a registrar post, but none were available in January 1969, so I went to the Royal National Throat, Nose, and Ear Hospital in Gray's Inn Road, the centre of ENT academia, as an SHO.[15] It was deemed almost essential to spend some time at Gray's Inn Road (GIR) so that not only could one become known to the powers that be (most of the GIR consultants also held posts at other London teaching hospitals) but also to acquaint oneself with the politics of the speciality.

After the civilisation of Barts, it was – to be brutally honest – a bit of a come-down, not surgically, I may add, but socially and domestically. A few days into my appointment, I met my former boss from Barts (he was also on the staff of GIR), who smiled sweetly: 'Hello, Douglas. Are you slumming it?' Despite being a graduate of St. Thomas', I felt very much an 'insider' at Barts, yet an 'outsider' at GIR. Nevertheless, it was a useful posting: I met loads of influential people, had good teaching (as a post-graduate

---

[15] The building is now closed, and its services are re-located at the rebuilt Royal Ear Hospital in Huntley Street.

institution, educational events were frequent), and gained a wide spectrum of clinical and operative experience. GIR also had a training scheme of two years spent as a registrar and one as a senior registrar, but this seemed a bit half-cock because one then had to enter the senior registrar market (*the* critical career progression) at the wrong stage. I also decided that I would prefer to train in a general hospital as I would see a greater variety of clinical material, particularly on ENT problems in 'non-ENT' patients.

There were four senior house officers (no real juniors below us to do the boring, dirty work!), so it was a one-in-four rota. There was no such thing as a pre-admission clinic, so we had to 'clerk' the patients, take consent, and take any necessary bloods – and, if we were lucky, get to operate on them.[16] Faced with a long line of recently-admitted healthy young adults waiting in their night clothes for tonsillectomy or nasal surgery, I enquired of one man about what he did for a living. 'A friar', he answered. Looking up from the notes, I asked, 'of fish?'. 'No', he said, 'I am a Franciscan.' 'Friar' and 'fryer' sound the same… I had to attend an outpatient clinic on Thursday evenings, a further clinic on Saturday mornings, and come in every Sunday afternoon to prepare the patients for Monday's operating list – and the Dean of the Institute still complained that we were 'always dashing home to do the washing' (it was not like that in his

---

[16] 'Clerking' is the process of taking a history, examining the patient, and writing it all down in the notes. It can be tedious.

day, of course). We were only in our mid-twenties, so we survived this rather 'non-compliant with the European Working Time Directive' timetable, but this was not only pre-EU; it was before the British entry into EEC!

Being attached to an otologist, fortunately, I was spared any substantial involvement in head and neck cancer surgery which again struck me as brutal and often imperceptive of the patient's needs, lifestyle, and (often) a poor prognosis. Otology was different: it was elegant, nearly always had a good outcome, and it was a joy to see patients discarding their hearing aids after a successful stapedectomy. The motto of GIR was *audient surdi, mutique loquentur* ('The deaf shall hear, the dumb shall speak'): we were more successful with the former than the latter, although it was appreciated (certainly by 1969) that dumbness was secondary to deafness. If you cannot hear, you cannot copy speech sounds. I became a dab hand at inserting grommets, but one of our very senior consultants disapproved of the procedure, preferring revision after revision of adenoidectomy in an attempt to improve Eustachian tube function. After one such performance with an over-large curette, I found that he had removed two little slivers of cartilage from the opening of the Eustachian tubes, four front teeth, and about two match-heads worth of adenoid. Hmm. Perhaps suction diathermy adenoidectomy is a substantial advance.

Epistaxis (nose bleeds) was, is, and ever shall be the bane of the duty ENT SHO. How many times were we called by the ENT house surgeon at ‘St. Elsewhere’s in the East End’ who had packed and repacked the nose, all to no avail? I was never quite sure what we could do, as ligation of external carotid arteries seemed a bit radical, and sphenopalatine artery clipping was way in the future. One consultant had a novel approach: no packs but just sedate the patient (with phenobarbitone, I think) so that he/she was practically unconscious with a lowered blood pressure in an attempt to arrest the bleeding. This struck me as being a questionable practice (I could feel the lawyers breathing down my neck), but how to deal with the situation? Simple: manage the patient conventionally but have two sets of notes. The first (the real notes) documented the correct management, and the second (a temporary file) could be shown to the boss on his ward round and then destroyed. Devious and unconventional, but I hope it saved lives: people have died from nosebleeds.

Curiously, I have virtually no memories of particular patients, although I do have a few memories of working at GIR. Outpatients took place in a large hall, with only the consultant’s room giving any degree of privacy: in terms of today, I suppose we just about managed ‘social distancing’ between the nine ‘workstations’ (not that either term existed in 1969) but one could certainly pick up snippets of the conversations at other tables. One registrar was clearly frustrated by his patient’s lack of perception of her condition as his voice boomed out across the room ‘Madam, I can’t do anything more for you. I suggest you take an aeroplane to Lourdes.' I like to think that our communication skills have improved in the last half-century, but, despite the endless psychobabble to which students are now subjected, I sometimes wonder: my generation was taught nothing about how to approach a patient, let alone convey bad news. I suppose I was at the tail end of the 'doctor knows best and don't you dare argue' era – especially if the doctor was a senior teaching hospital consultant with a very smart suit, stiff collar, and large private practice. On the other hand, I do recall an East Ender saying to me, 'My doctor, like. He's an iggorant pig of a man, is my doctor'. Actually, I rather agreed with him but did not say so.

GIR was a small hospital by modern standards, and the night portering staff was restricted to one man, who sat at the front door, ran any necessary errands, and operated the telephone switchboard. Late one evening, I needed the duty anaesthetist for some emergency procedure but could get no response from the switchboard. Undeterred, I walked to the front hall to find the duty porter fast asleep and slumped over the switchboard. At least he was sober.

As I have said, I went to GIR as a stopgap pending a registrar job, so on Friday mornings, I would rush to the library (the clinic could wait – nobody was ever seen on time!) to look at the advertisements in *The British Medical Journal*. Two jobs were advertised one morning in early April: St. Thomas' Hospital and The London Hospital. To cut a long story filled with political machinations short, I was appointed registrar at The London from 1 June, leaving the hallowed walls of GIR a month before my allotted date.

But there were other ways to escape the clutches of The Royal National Throat, Nose, and Ear Hospital. The hospital had a second branch (again, now closed) in Golden Square behind Regent Street and within easy striking distance of the Piccadilly Circus tube station: I made occasional visits there for teaching purposes. One morning prior to a routine Ts & As list, the ward nurses observed a small boy clad only in pyjamas running flat out across Golden Square in the direction of Piccadilly Circus…

Chapter 7

ENT Registrar, The London Hospital

A registrar appointment was effectively the beginning of a surgical career: the previous appointments of House Officer and Senior House Officer led the newly-qualified doctor through a highly-supervised (sometimes) first year, with six months in medicine and six in surgery. After this baptism by fire, one was 'fully registered' with the General Medical Council and could work in hospitals, general practice, the armed forces, or industry and, if staying in hospital practice, one became a Senior House Officer (SHO) with increasing responsibility, and, for the surgeons, more operating (hooray!). The intending specialist undertook jobs in his or her chosen specialty and, in the case of surgeons, sat the Primary FRCS examination.[17]

As a registrar, one was definitely a fledgling surgeon with greater clinical responsibility, supervising the juniors as well as receiving tuition, doing clinical work, being on-call, and studying (and studying and studying). In my time, we took the final FRCS examination after at least a year as a registrar: the possession of the FRCS deemed us suitable to undertake higher surgical training, and it did feel good to become Mr MacMillan rather than the common Dr

---

[17] Fellowship of the Royal College of Surgeons.

MacMillan. I found, however, that it was easier to revert to 'Dr' when the car needed urgent repairs… Following about two years as a registrar, we had to jump the biggest hurdle in training to become a senior registrar: thereafter, a consultancy was almost inevitable. Nowadays, the FRCS is taken towards the end of speciality training to indicate suitability for a consultant appointment.[18]

So in June 1969, it was back to the East End, alighting from the tube at Whitechapel to cross the Whitechapel Road and enter The London Hospital (now The Royal London Hospital), another maze of a building with its own character. I'm not sure what it is like in our rather standardised and levelled-down era, but fifty years ago, each teaching hospital carried a wealth of traditions unique to itself (I have already said much about Barts), and it took a few weeks to crack the system. The nurses' uniforms were quite distinctive: at The London, the dresses were midi-length with mutton-leg sleeves, and aprons were worn without a belt. On state occasions, sisters had two long 'tails' attached to their cap, but there was considerably less obscure jargon than at the much-older Barts. The operating theatres were, shall we say, 'of their time' with no air conditioning: doing a long operation on a July day with a theatre temperature of over 90 degrees Fahrenheit (about 33 Celsius) was grim, and nobody

[18] The current training involves two years as a foundation doctor (FY1 and FY2), two years as a core surgical trainee (CST- equivalent to an SHO), followed by about six years of speciality training, the equivalent of being a registrar and, subsequently, a senior registrar.

ever thought of stopping for (non-alcoholic!) fluid replenishment. The out-patient department, like Gray's Inn Road, showed little respect for privacy, but, remember, we were less sensitive about such basic human rights in 1969. There were three consultants in the department, two senior registrars, and two registrars, so a one-in-four on-call rota was a welcome relief. We also had three hearing aid technicians who inhabited their own little world and one audiologist who worked in a very hot, totally enclosed room and emerged from time to time looking like the archetypical beetroot.

I was delighted to return to the East End: my old stamping-ground of Mile End Hospital was just over a mile away, and during my time as a registrar, Mile End was taken under the wing of The London, so I returned to the operating theatres were I had performed my first Ts & As. Whitechapel remained characterful: I remember seeing a horse drinking the slops of beer whilst tied up at a pub near the hospital while its owner refreshed himself within. Naturally enough, we saw a large number of children with tonsil problems: many a time, a small, snotty child would be shoved in front of a surgeon by its mother ''e keeps getting tonsillitis, and I want 'is tonsils out''. The converse presentation ran "e keeps on getting tonsillitis but I ain't 'aving 'is tonsils out''. I suppose we surgeons were allowed to make the decision in about a third of the cases: whatever else one says about the

East Enders, they certainly had firm and determined attitudes to life, but, as I have said before, they had hearts of gold.

Talking of Ts & As reminds me of Brentwood Hospital. During the Second World War, all the London teaching hospitals had a satellite hospital out of town for the performance of elective surgery away from the threat of bombing in central London, and these remained active for some years after the war had ended. Barts had Hill End near St. Albans, Thomas's a unit at Hydestile in Surrey, and The London operated at Brentwood, some 20 miles to the east. After the Friday morning clinic, a couple of registrars, usually accompanied by the boss, would climb into their cars to operate at Brentwood. We did not get to see the cases before operation: most were fairly minor procedures, and the duty first-year house surgeon had pronounced them fit for surgery (how he knew, I'm not sure) in the war-time theatre, which had two operating tables. So far, so good: most operations are straightforward and complication free, but anything to do with tonsils carries a small risk of post-operative bleeding. Nevertheless, we went straight back to London after the list, leaving the care of the patients in the hands of the very junior house surgeon. How we got away with this amazes me: the very thought of driving back to Brentwood in a hurry from somewhere in London on a Friday evening filled me with dread, but nothing catastrophic happened, at least on my watch. The gods must have been on the side of the surgeons – or the children!

Fortunately, my principal boss was an otologist (ear surgeon), so I again escaped much involvement in head and neck cancer surgery. One curious relic of past otology should be recorded, that of homograft tympanoplasty, the replacement of the ear drum and/or middle ear bones by a graft harvested from a cadaver. This, of course, was in the days before HIV and AIDS and substantially before much concern was raised about Hepatitis B, and I do not recall consent being obtained for the removal of tissue from the cadaver. We registrars benefitted from the experience of preparing the grafts, a tricky exercise in micro-surgery, but the procedure itself failed to show any great degree of success and was soon abandoned.

A practice popular in the late 1960s and early '70s was hormonal ablation surgery to attempt to control the pain of patients with widespread breast cancer, and ENT surgeons became involved when it was discovered that the pituitary gland, a major producer of all sorts of hormones dangling from the base of the brain could be approached via the nose. This approach was far less invasive than a neurosurgical procedure, and, as most of the patients were already very seriously ill, it became the preferred operation. I do recall that many of these poor ladies probably had only weeks to live, and I really wondered at the time if we were justified in offering this procedure: the results were unpredictable, but some patients did obtain some relief from bone pain. The operation (technically known as trans-sphenoidal hypophysectomy) fell out of favour for this particular condition, but the nasal approach to the pituitary continues to be employed for other conditions.

One 'speciality' of the department was the removal of acoustic neuromas, an uncommon benign tumour of the hearing nerve which was formerly removed by an extensive neurosurgical procedure, but my boss and his neurosurgical colleague were early advocates of its removal through the ear combined with a craniotomy. This very long operation was a substantial advance and left the patients with less residual disability.

There is no doubt that ENT is a very 'medical' speciality, and only a small percentage of our patients end up on the operating table. As a young registrar, I was a bit disappointed by this, but as my career developed, I became more and more fascinated by 'medical ENT', particularly in regard to nasal disease and allergy, and also the investigation and management of dizzy patients. By the end of my career, I could almost describe myself more as an ENT physician rather than an ENT surgeon! Ménière's Disease (a nasty condition with severe giddy attacks, hearing loss, and tinnitus) was managed by a curious combination of rather ineffective drugs: some of these were basically antihistamines with 'anti-giddy' side-effects (you can still buy some of them for travel sickness) but, because they were antihistaminic, people thought that Ménière's was an allergy-based disease. We did some pharmacology at medical school but much evidently fell on the ears of sleeping undergraduates in the lecture theatre.... There was no logic in attempting to blame allergy for Mons. Ménière's disease.

After my first year as a registrar, I passed my final FRCS examination in the briefest allowed time after qualification and on my first attempt (about 5% passed the first time), and, of course, I felt that I had really arrived on the surgical scene! Now formally addressed as 'Mr MacMillan,' I suppose I thought the surgical world was my oyster. My father, an exceptionally generous man, offered to buy me a present to celebrate my FRCS: I think he was surprised when I asked for a new treble recorder rather than surgical instruments but, as we shall see, this would be the shape of things to come. There is one other tale to tell about ear disease before I continue with what we would now call my 'career pathway', and that case is about a patient with nerve deafness caused by syphilis.

As an undergrad, I remember seeing patients stumping down the corridor of St. Thomas's Hospital with the classical 'stamping gate' of tertiary syphilis, but it was only as an ENT registrar that I had to have any dealings with this horrible – if absolutely fascinating – disease which could cause severe nerve deafness. The condition was still prevalent all those years ago, and blood tests for syphilis were a standard part of the work-up of many conditions, including nerve deafness. One morning I had to impart to a deaf patient that he had an abnormal blood test (we did not tell them much in those days), and he would have to be referred to the Genito-Urinary Medicine clinic euphemistically referred to at The London as the 'Special Clinic'.[19] Never should we try to pull the wool over a patient's eyes: the man looked at me and said, 'Doc, I've been a seaman all my life, and I know I have been a bad boy. I know what your Special Clinic is for'. The treatment (which I think occasionally worked to some degree) consisted of steroids plus four (yes, four!) injections of penicillin a day for at least a week. Whether anyone could sit on a hard chair for a month after this posterior battering is doubtful.

By six months after passing my FRCS, I began to wonder if surgery was really for me: I suppose I had hoped for more operating and more complex procedures now that I held the magic diploma of FRCS, but it seemed that there was little change in my work pattern, although I no longer had to spend every evening 'bashing the books'. This allowed me – at last – to develop my musical interests, which were becoming increasingly focused on the recorder and Baroque music. At work, I was not really exposed to the practice of the medical ENT ((allergy and balance disorders), which became such a part of my subsequent career, but I was developing a deep

---

[19] Formerly called the Venereal Disease Clinic, or, more colloquially, the Clap Clinic, although for some unaccountable reason the department was called 'Lydia' at St. Thomas's!

interest in palliative care (in those days called terminal care). This, I think, was stimulated by hearing Cicely Saunders speak on several occasions at St. Thomas's, by the story of Mrs A at Brighton, and the primitive approach to pain relief in the dying. Once a patient was started on 'Brompton Mixture', they were substantially written off by many medical teams, and my experience of our poor pituitary removal patients made me reflect deeply on how appalling the care was for people in their last few months or weeks of their life.[20]

I was beginning to think that my medical future lay in palliative care medicine rather than surgery and decided to break with hospital medicine for some experience in general practice. Inevitably, this was a difficult decision and, in retrospect, completely wrong.

---

[20] The Brompton Cocktail was a mixture of morphine or heroin, cocaine, pure alcohol (or neat gin) and chloroform water.

Chapter 8

Into the wilderness 2

General Practice

Perhaps the subtitle of this chapter should read 'when I swapped my white coat for a tweed jacket!' One dull morning in November 1969, I climbed into my Morris Minor ('Mildred') for the six-mile drive to what was euphemistically described as 'sunny Southfields', a lower middle-/upper working-class district of Wimbledon in south London. It is fair to comment that I was a little less than enthusiastic about the job, but, equally, I was determined to make the most of the new experience: I should indicate that, in my five years at medical school, I was offered no experience in general practice despite the fact that about a third of doctors become GPs.

By modern standards, the practice was small. There were four partners, a trainee (me), a nurse, and a scattering of receptionists, and, unlike modern-day general practice, the partners were not supported by a plethora of part-time doctors. We had the main surgery and two branch surgeries and took it in turns to be on call, but after a certain hour in the evening, calls were switched to a call service that provided doctors to cover any necessary advice or visits – so I never had to get out of bed to chase around south London in the middle of the night. It is one thing to drive to one's hospital at three in the morning but quite another to navigate around a tower-block estate with its unreliable lifts and filthy staircases, but I never recall being physically threatened. Times have changed for out-of-hours GPs who now appear to have a driver – and some degree of protection afforded by their presence. On one late evening visit in the dark, I was surprised to find myself in front of a Mosque and did wonder if I was hallucinating: however, the Fazl Mosque was indeed real and the first Mosque to be built in London.

I recall a story about a consultant physician and a GP who met up for a beer after their day's work. The physician (no doubt in his three-piece suit) asked the GP (in his tweed jacket and brown shoes) if he had seen any interesting cases that day. As quick as a flash, our kindly family doctor answered, 'No, but I have seen a lot of interesting people'. I think that apparently trivial story summed it up for me: I certainly cared about my patients, but I needed some decent clinical material (!) to engage my interest. However, the moment a patient became really interesting or exciting, they were whisked off to the hospital, and I missed all the fun. As an ex-hospital doctor, I was horrified by the relatively infrequent use of blood tests, X-rays, and other investigations in general practice. We had only one ECG machine between the three surgeries… The GPs relied far more on clinical experience than I did (or indeed had!) as a junior hospital doctor, and I lived in fear of medical negligence actions, despite having been ticked off by one of the partners for ordering some X-rays on a patient who had sustained a head injury, as was standard practice in Casualty.

Most of the work was solid clinical medicine, but another factor began to rear its ugly head in the form of psychological interpretation. My time as a GP coincided with a rise of enthusiasm for Michael Balint's *The Doctor, the Patient, and his Illness*, which, although profoundly thoughtful, could lead to making simple things complicated – not in the temperament of surgeons. One wet Monday morning in November, I was sitting in the surgery with my trainer when a young man hobbled in, having hurt his ankle at football the previous Saturday. The GP strapped up his ankle and put him off games for a week: as an ex-Casualty Officer, I would have reached for an X-ray request form. There then followed an intriguing dialogue:

Trainer	Why do you think he sprained his ankle?
DM	He told you: he was playing football on Saturday.
Trainer	Yes, but any particular reason why he should have hurt himself?
DM	Well, it was raining, and the pitch would have been muddy and slippery.
Trainer	No, something else?
DM	(exasperated) A young man hurts his ankle playing football on a muddy field. Isn't that enough reason? What are you thinking of?

Trainer Perhaps he had had a row with his girlfriend and was more likely to fall…

In the hands of experienced doctors, clinical medicine is one thing, but this?

Since I was deemed to be more experienced than many GP trainees, I was left largely to my own devices to get on with the job. Surgeries were then, as now, a mixture of the trivial, the unnecessary, and serious illness: the former two prevailed, which rather frustrated me. There was no such thing as a repeat prescription service, so patients would call in every few weeks to see a doctor just for a new prescription of their routine medication, an incredible waste of medical time. Back in 1970, a patient could only 'self-certify' to be absent from work for a period of up to three days before needing a medical sick certificate (it is now seven days). If you think about it, most minor illnesses get better in a week (colds, sore throats, tummy bugs, and minor injuries), and we spent much time writing seemingly unnecessary 'sick notes': however, some employers would not accept the NHS note and insisted on a private certificate – for which we were entitled to charge a fee. I do recall that the fee recommended by the British Medical Association for this service was 10s 6d (about £7.50 today), a ridiculous sum in relation to the average earnings in Southfields. Usually, I just signed the chit and gave it to the patient, much to the wrath of my superiors – but it was I who missed out on the cash!

After morning surgery, each doctor would be given a list of house calls, probably six to eight in the winter months. I began to realise how difficult it was to practise thorough clinical medicine away from the surgery, particularly with elderly patients who had difficulty undressing for chest or abdominal examination. The converse, of course, is that it made life easier for the infirm and elderly, and it should be recalled that not everyone in Southfields owned a car: indeed, a former GP told me that in the early 1970s, many people gave up driving at the age of 70 anyway!

There is no doubt that the privilege of entering peoples' homes taught me much about the way of life of different socio-economic groups. I would hesitate to use the phrase 'living in squalor', but it is fair to say that the standard of basic domestic hygiene sometimes horrified me. Medical School had not prepared me for this, nor had it prepared me for the difficulty of listening through a stethoscope with the inevitable TV (usually black and white) blaring in the background to keep the kids quiet. However, one delightful Italian family always offered me a slice or two of *Mordatella*, some olives, and a glass of wine when I called. Fortunately (for me), a fortnightly visit was required…and usually timed as my last call of the morning.

On the other hand, there were real gut-wrenching visits. One morning I was called to an elderly lady who had not been seen in the practice for some time and who was complaining of breathlessness. She looked horribly ill, and I was thinking 'pneumonia'. Not so. I needed to listen to her chest, and she unbuttoned her shirt slowly. I can recall to this day the sight and smell of an enormous fungating and untreated breast cancer. Poor lady: she was just too frightened to go to the doctor at a stage when her disease could possibly have been cured. I could only hope that she had a peaceful end, as there was nothing any doctor could have done except palliate her symptoms.

As the months rolled on, it was becoming increasingly apparent that I was not suited to being a GP (I suspect that my colleagues would have agreed!), and I resolved to re-enter the career race-track, which was surgery. To say the least of it, this was an unusual move in the career of a young doctor: once one had exited the ivory tower of the teaching hospitals, there was little chance of re-entry. Never one to let convention stand in my way, I surreptitiously scanned my trainer's copy of the *British Medical Journal* and found that an ENT registrar was required at Barts and so I made a few 'phone calls to my old boss, submitted an application form, and took the tube to Barts to have a friendly chat with the consultants for whom I had worked a couple of years earlier. On 1 July 1971, 'I came back as a registrar' to my medical spiritual home.

Many years on, I still ask myself, 'should I have stepped out of ENT when I did?' Realistically, the answer is an unequivocal 'no', but I was blessed with good fortune and returned to ENT with a massive sense of relief at coming home. On my first afternoon as a registrar, the boss offered to let me do the first tonsillectomy on the list – I had not forgotten how to operate! Although my time in general practice was far from agreeable, I have absolutely no doubt that it made me a better doctor, particularly with regard to looking at the social factors underlying illness and just seeing, in the raw, how people lived, moved, and had their being outside of teaching hospitals and upper-middle-class values. At the end of the day, we are all just examples of *Homo sapiens,* although, to quote George Orwell, 'All animals are equal, but some animals are more equal than others'. The evident truth of his aphorism is vividly laid out before the general medical practitioner.

Chapter 9
ENT Registrar and locum Senior Registrar, St. Bartholomew's Hospital
Part 1: registrar

Three years after my first week at Barts as a house surgeon, I felt immensely privileged to walk once more into the hallowed walls of this ancient hospital: I was back to a familiar landscape, to familiar jargon, and to working with consultants whom I had known (and who, no doubt, knew me). Life had certainly taken a turn for the better when I put on my white coat again! I am not sure to this day how I managed to acquire two jobs at Barts without so much as an interview, but I have my ideas, which remain absolutely 'non-disclosable'!

Not only was I back in familiar territory, but also, by the time I returned to Barts, I had already gained eighteen months' experience as a registrar at The London, so I knew my way around the basic repertoire of ENT operations. The normal duration of working in the registrar grade was about two years, so in that sense (and armed with my FRCS), I was well on the way to a Senior Registrar appointment – of which, more later. We worked a one-in-three on-call rota (a registrar and two senior registrars), but as the City of London had a minute residential population, night calls were (thankfully!) a rarity. Like all young surgeons, we complained that we did not get enough operating, but by today's standards, we were living in operating clover and often left to our own devices in the theatre (for better or worse) far more than today's trainees. The consultants, without exception, took their training responsibilities seriously, and I was gradually inducted into middle ear and neck surgery.

With our tiny resident population in The City, our beds were largely free from the emergency, which bedevilled most ENT departments, namely severe nose-bleeds, but to compensate, we made a good trade in broken noses. On the opposite side of Smithfield Rotunda Garden lay the (now closed) Smithfield Meat Market and a pub that opened early in the morning for the night shift porters to refresh themselves before rolling home. It was a common occurrence for the porters to come into nasal contact with huge sides of beef, and inevitably, the availability of alcohol even early in the morning produced its share of fist-fights. At least we could operate on their broken noses!

When I was a houseman at Barts, I was intrigued to see that one of the consultants had an outpatient session on Wednesday afternoons (he operated on Wednesday mornings) designated as 'allergy and calorics', but it was only after I became his registrar that I was initiated into the mysteries of this clinic. Allergy seemed fairly straightforward: I had suffered from hay fever for years, and

I was pleased to find that someone as high-powered as a Barts consultant was taking this disabling condition seriously. The experience of attending a homeopathic practitioner in my 'teens left much to be desired… The patients underwent skin prick testing to confirm or deny any allergic involvement in their nasal symptoms and were sometimes prescribed a series of desensitising injections, which, in many cases, produced good results. However, a series of disasters – usually caused by practitioners who were not aware of the risks of the treatment – led to desensitisation being banned. This was total bureaucratic overkill, for, in the hands of trained practitioners who were aware of the risks and knew how to manage any problems, it was a good treatment. Needless to say, the procedure has been refined, improved, and has come back into fashion.

The other facet of the Wednesday afternoon clinic – calorics – was concerned with the investigation of giddy patients. In simple terms, the ears were irrigated with warm and cold water to induce short-lived dizzy episodes, and the response of the two ears was compared. Realistically it was not fun for the patients (how many medical procedures are – but do we doctors appreciate this?) and boring to do, but it was a useful test and has yet to be supplanted.

Although 'allergy and calorics' are a long way from operative surgery, they underline that the ENT surgeon is often more of a physician than a surgeon: the assessment of much nasal disease is related to allergy, and very few dizzy patients end up on the operating table (at least for their dizziness!). I have emphasised Wednesday afternoons as this rather obscure and physicianly clinic kindled my interest in both allergy and neuro-otology, two disciplines that were destined to become bedrocks of my subsequent career. It could cynically be observed that neither snotty noses nor dizzy attacks rouse the on-call ENT surgeon from his bed…

Much of the character of Barts has been extolled in a previous chapter, so I think now is the point to take a little break from surgery and talk about music. The FRCS was done and dusted, so I no longer had to spend very available hours bashing the books for the exam and could begin to concentrate on the real love of my life, music. Eventually (curious though it sounds), music was to dominate my future surgical career, but for now, I had to be content with being very much an amateur recorder player. I had played the recorder and clarinet at school as well as conducting the orchestra, but in London, there was a plethora of clarinettists, so I was unable to get a second clarinet chair in an amateur orchestra. As I have noted, my musical tastes were becoming firmly rooted in the Baroque, music for which the recorder was eminently suitable, and it was a soft instrument unlikely to irritate the neighbours! The beautiful plumwood treble recorder which my father gave me on passing my FRCS became my constant stimulus and companion, and I knew that somehow or other, surgery and music had to become a stable marriage – but, of this, much more later. While a registrar at Barts, I do recall asking the boss if he would mind my being a few minutes late for the clinic one afternoon 'because I had to collect an instrument'. When I arrived back with a bass recorder, the only comment was, 'Oh! I thought you meant a surgical instrument'. *Ars longa, vita brevis*.[21]

Back in the early 1970s, the real career jump was between registrar (a two-year appointment with about 150 posts in England) and senior registrar (held for about four years and about 50 posts). Some trainees from overseas went back to their home countries after gaining their FRCS, but, for the rest of us, it became an exercise in creeping to the right people, working in the best departments, and filling out umpteen unsuccessful application forms. Once a senior registrar, one was virtually assured of a consultant post. I managed to slip into the senior registrar grade at Barts by means of a long locum appointment to replace a man who had taken a year out on a research fellowship but, of course, I still had to find a substantive senior registrar job. The grade was abolished in the Calman training reforms of the 1990s, although I think this was a big mistake. As a senior registrar, the trainee was carefully groomed for a consultancy, given a huge degree of clinical autonomy, and inducted into the administrative side of medicine: on a personal level, on appointment as a senior registrar, one felt that one had definitely gone up a rank in the hierarchy and was treated as

---

[21] 'Art is long, life is short'. I added this at the end of my undergraduate anatomy exam, which is probably why I failed.

a figure with seniority and authority, to my mind an excellent preparation for being the boss!

Part 2: locum Senior Registrar

In those days, Barts had two senior registrars in ENT, both of whom spent a day or two a week in other hospitals to undertake more specialised training. One senior registrar went to the Royal Marsden Hospital for training in head and neck cancer surgery, the other to the National Hospital for Nervous Diseases (now the National Hospital for Neurology and Neurosurgery) in Queen Square to learn to manage inner ear disorders, particularly dizzy patients. Mercifully I was assigned to Queen Square: as has no doubt become apparent during these pages, I could never really develop any enthusiasm for often mammoth and disfiguring cancer operations with their poor prognosis.

Off I went to that erudite bastion of neurological learning, Queen Square, without the slightest notion of how to diagnose and treat dizzy patients. My predecessor said it was easy 'Just fill out the questionnaire you will be given with each patient, and all will become crystal clear'. He was wrong – and after I retired 42 years later with vast experience in managing dizzy patients, it could still remain a mystery. Perhaps the challenge appealed to the speculating philosophical physician within me rather than the dynamic surgeon… The neuro-otology clinic was located in a dingey basement, and I recall spending hours making patients dizzy during caloric testing, an activity now carried out by audiology technicians. I also remember falling asleep during the boss' tutorial after a long clinic on a November afternoon. Anyway, it was a good experience, and I returned to Barts to take a greater interest in 'allergy and calorics' and seemed to become the resident enthusiast for both snotty noses and giddy patients. I do not think anyone else in the department had worked out how to drive the electronystagmograph machine, let alone interpret the results.[22] 'What exactly do you mean by dizzy?' I asked of one patient. 'Well, doc, it goes round and round in yer 'ead and then stops, dunnit!' I have asked every dizzy patient I have ever seen the same question, but never since have I received such an obfuscating answer. I do love the East Enders.

Operative surgery became more fascinating and challenging, and I was particularly attracted to microsurgery of the ear and (perversely) nasal surgery, probably because nobody else seemed interested in the latter. As a senior registrar, one was allowed to plough into uncharted waters without constant consultant supervision, not perhaps a good plan in terms of risk management. I found myself having to drain a frontal sinus, so I just booked a theatre and an anaesthetist, read the book and got on with it: I had seen it done once at Mile End five years before. There is an old

---

[22] A machine which records the eye movements in dizzy patients, usually during caloric testing.

maxim about surgical training, 'see one, do one, teach one,' and it was not entirely untrue in my training days. It does not apply nowadays!

During all this fascinating clinical activity, one thought kept 'running in the background': getting a senior registrar post. I answered advertisements for several suitable posts, including one at my old medical school at Thomas's: at the interview, I was greeted by the Dean of the Medical School with the words 'Well, MacMillan, you appear to have been on a Cook's tour of London teaching hospitals'.[23] I could have answered, 'that's because you never gave me a job here', but thought the better of it. Eventually, I was appointed to University College Hospital, whose ENT department was regarded as a bit behind the times and in need of a catalytic conversion to modernity. In December 1972, I left my beloved Barts behind to take on a new challenge – but with a tear in my eye.

[23] Mary's, Barts, The London, Grays Inn Road, and Queen Square.

Chapter 10

Chief Assistant, The Royal Ear Hospital

The ENT Department of University College Hospital was housed in a rather elegant 1930s building in Huntley Street, The Royal Ear Hospital. Now demolished to make way for a shiny new Royal National Throat, Nose, and Ear Hospital (ex Gray's Inn Road), it was connected to the next-door obstetric hospital and the parent UCH by a sinuous underground corridor. As a small self-contained unit, we enjoyed the familiarity of a village hospital attached to the formidable resources of a London Teaching Hospital, and as senior registrar, I was styled 'Chief Assistant', a title which has long since passed into history. I had an office (the walls of which were soon festooned with prints of Renaissance art) and essentially ran the place as soon as I had asserted my seniority as a Fellow of the Royal College of Surgeons over a protocol-befixed nursing sister (more later!). We were four consultants (all part-time, some 'very'), two senior registrars (myself and a part-timer), two registrars, and two pre-registration (FY1) housemen with a remarkable four-tier on-call rota of houseman, registrar, senior registrar, and consultant. As a senior registrar, I was seldom troubled whilst on duty: this was fortunate because I could be on call for four weeks at a stretch!

Apart from the routine clinical work (I had my own operating list once a week and also assisted the consultants in theatre for experience and training), I planned the admissions, administered the undergraduate teaching programme (which was great fun), and amongst other responsibilities, my contract stated that I was responsible for 'the suckers at the Royal Ear Hospital'. To this day, I am not sure whether this referred to various mechanical devices or the people who were sufficient suckers to work for the NHS…

Given that the reputation of the department was that it was old-fashioned, as a dynamic, forward-thinking senior registrar, I made it my prime agenda to make the Royal Ear Hospital once more a bastion of ENT modernity, and inevitably in this exercise, I was massively influenced by Barts. However, I foresaw that conflicts and storms would lie on the horizon: no conservative institution takes kindly to change, however logical it may be. I arrived on a Monday morning to find the two registrars wandering around the wards like the blind leading the partially paralysed, followed by two somewhat-disinterested housemen: life appeared to be dictated by a series of protocols established many moons before the 1970s and still faithfully and dutifully enacted by the junior staff. This had to change. After minor nasal operations, the hospital stay was decreed to be five days: after one-side radical sinus operations, it would be five days, but if both sides were done, ten days. One registrar caustically observed that it was fortunate that mankind did not have five major sinuses… Needless to say, I relegated all this antiquated nonsense to the rubbish bin (remember that minor nasal procedures are now performed as 'day cases') and discharged a man two days after his op. He was fit, could easily go home to his loving wife, and might as well put up with his blocked snotty nose for a few days in his own home and spare the NHS a bed (yes, there were bed shortages in 1972!) Shortly afterward, I was assailed by the senior nursing sister 'Mr. MacMillan, you sent a man home two days after a nasal operation: they are required to stay for five days'. 'Yes, sister, but he was fit to be discharged'. Good sporting stuff: I won. I also managed to incur the wrath of someone (I can't remember who it was) who kindly thought I would like to do a middle ear operation on my first Wednesday list: nice thought, but I had to send the man home because his teeth were so rotten that he would have been a risk to the anaesthetist. Start as you mean to go on, DM.

During my first weeks, I also re-organised the departmental museum (a useful experience for a man who was to spend much of his retirement working in musical instrument museums!), revised the undergraduate teaching programme, and probably irritated everyone except the registrars, who were delighted to have a constructive senior to supervise them. By the time of the Royal Ear Hospital (REH)'s celebrated Christmas party, I felt that I was bedded in. The Christmas party was interesting: the boss asked, 'should we invite the Professor of Medicine?' DM: 'Why?' Boss: 'Don't know. Who is he anyway?' Regardless of the presence or absence of the Professor of Medicine (or Surgery, or Pathology, or anything else), it was a good party, and I looked forward to getting to grips with more complex operations in 1973.

With my interest in inner ear disorders such as Ménière's Disease growing, I should mention some of the older operations for this condition which is now very amenable to drug treatment or minor interventions in the out-patient department. Before getting into the minutiae of these operations, it is well to reflect that, back in the early 1970s, some surgeons still opened the mastoid in the manner time-hallowed by their predecessors, namely with a mallet and gouge instead of the more controllable and accurate drill. The 'old masters' were reputed to have been able to perform a mastoid operation in 40 minutes with a hammer and gouge using the unaided human eyeball: it now takes some hours using a drill and microscope, but the results nowadays are vastly better and the previously 'not uncommon' complications almost nil. But back to Ménière's Disease: I will not bore you with most of the operations, save to mention the very radical 'osseous labyrinthectomy, which involved total destruction of the offending ear and the quaint and crazy Cody Tack operation. Labyrinthectomy inevitably left the patient with no hearing in the operated ear and usually persistent tinnitus and poor balance, so more conservative measures were conceived. In Ménière's, there is an excess of inner ear fluid, so the system swells up: part of the inner ear (the saccule, for the technically minded) lies directly under the stirrup bone (stapes) of the middle ear, and it occurred to a number of otologists that puncturing the saccule would release the pressure in the inner ear. Cody proposed placing a tiny tack about 2mm long in the stapes so that, when the patient had a giddy attack, and the saccule swelled, the tack would puncture the sac and terminate the attack. Lovely thought, but of course, it did not work, and the process of inserting the tack was tricky, to say the least of it. I think I lost five tacks in someone's middle ear in the process. He was none the worse for the presence of loose micro-ironmongery left in his ear, but his Ménière's was no better…

Nowadays, a surgeon is (quite rightly) expected to have attended training and observed other surgeons before adding a new operation to his or her repertoire. In my training days, the old maxim of 'see one, do one, teach one' applied, and even the 'see one' was often omitted! As a senior registrar, I believe I was the only person at the REH at the time to have performed a Moure's lateral rhinotomy and a laryngofissure, both quite substantial and now out-dated operations. It was in the books, so what need of a tutor – but I do not think we were as aware of lawyers as today's surgeons, and risk management practice and audit were way in the future. But then, patients were not so ready to call their solicitor after any minor (or even major) surgical mishap…

Just a final note on dizziness before a quick look at deafness in kids: I have already mentioned the caloric test, irrigating the ears with water to test balance function, which is an unpleasant experience for the patient and boring for the doctor to perform. It so happened that my tenure as senior registrar coincided with the long hot, dry summer of 1976, and to protect the water supply under drought conditions, a notice appeared above the caloric test equipment 'No calorics without permission of the senior registrar'. Very environmentally friendly, but as I did most of the calorics, it was not entirely altruistic…

But let us get back to more commonplace ENT – hearing problems. We made a good trade in grommet insertions, to my mind, an excellent procedure to tide kids over while they grow out of their glue ears: there is absolutely no doubt that normal hearing is essential not only in the classroom but in the social development of children. Would you rather your child had a simple, painless, and effective operation (ten minutes!) or attempt to persuade them to wear a hearing aid – bearing in mind that it was only in the early 1970s that 'behind the ear' aids became available? The older 'plug, wire, box' body-worn aids were cumbersome, to say the least of it. One of the curious spin-offs of my job (although certainly not in the job description!) was to act as an audiological consultant to two Partial Hearing Units, units which were attached to a normal school and attended by pupils with substantial hearing loss, most wearing hearing aids. It should be noted that these units were far from 'deaf schools' using sign language and were intended to aid the integration of the children into a normal hearing world. The kids received special tuition from Teachers of the Deaf for the more complex subjects but were integrated into normal classes with normal hearing children in others. Certainly, this experience (like most of my more peripheral ENT activities) taught me much about social problems and allowed me to interact on a professional level with teachers, schools, social workers, and parents. Coffee in the school staff room provided a useful background to my subsequent musical career, which at one time included teaching the recorder in a boys' preparatory school…

At this point, I should return to my increasing obsession with music. In 1973 I attended a recorder summer school and came into contact with some very significant musicians in the form of the Dolmetsch family. On returning to the REH, I remembered that the University of London's Music Library was only a few minutes from the hospital, and I sallied forth to do some research and write an academic article on the crumhorn: my only previous research training had been in the gynaecology department at Thomas's, but nevertheless the die was cast as my paper was accepted in a leading musicological journal. I had recently founded a chamber ensemble, the Oriana Consort, and was intending to take a diploma in music: one Friday lunch-time, I was practising my scales on the recorder in a sound-treated room in the audiology department and was quite miffed when the boss summoned me to do a laryngectomy…

In those far-off days, nasal disease and its treatment (the subject of rhinology) were definitely the least favoured part of ear, nose, and throat surgery: the operations were (at least compared to the present day) on the brutal side and had hardly evolved for decades. I was fortunate to be timetabled to attend an allergy clinic once a week which was run by a highly intelligent (and musical!) consultant in allergy and respiratory medicine. I suspect that it was during this time that I realised that the ENT world had been 'barking up the wrong tree', seeing nasal disease as a surgical problem, whereas I increasingly saw it as a medical problem with the root cause being an unstable nasal lining, and as the nasal equivalent of asthma. It is easy enough to correct bony defects causing a blocked nose, but quite another matter to deal with the unstable nasal lining: we all experience problems with the lining of our noses when we get colds or hay fever, but chronic nasal disease is quite a debilitating condition. It is here that the parallel with asthma appears, for the lining of the nose and the bronchi are continuous parts of our airways.

Enter inhaled steroids in the form of beconase and becotide! Before the days of inhaled steroids in the early 1970s, many asthmatics had to take steroids by mouth, with their attendant risks and side-effects: some severe asthmatics took so much steroid that they suffered from osteoporosis (thinned weak bones), and it was even said that turning in bed could cause a patient to break a rib. This was something of an exaggeration, but you will get my point! Dumping the steroid straight onto the bronchi by inhalation massively reduced the need for steroid tablets, and a little later, inhaled steroids became the treatment of choice for most cases of rhinitis. I think it may be difficult for those who trained after the 1970s to appreciate the massive role inhaled steroids play in the management of respiratory disease: they have certainly made a great difference to my previous hay fever-ridden summers! There was also an added benefit for us hungry-to-operate young surgeons: when the asthmatics came off their steroid pills, their nasal disease ceased to be controlled, and we made a great trade in whipping out nasal polyps – at least until our fun was spoilt by the advent of steroids sprayed into the nose.

It was while working with the allergist in the Tuesday afternoon clinics that I became fascinated by allergy: investigation of allergic disease is a Poirot-like exercise in small-print detection! I was always a 'very medically-minded surgeon', not seeing the knife as a cure for all maladies, and, indeed, allergy became a dominant feature of my work. Taking long, detailed histories about the family history, the patient's home, work, and environment followed by simple, effective, safe, and reliable skin prick testing proved an increasing fascination which, I suppose, began with ‘allergy and calorics’ afternoons at Barts and led ultimately to my permanent appointment at Guildford.

Mentioning a visit to the ENT clinic for nasal problems invokes in the minds of many older people the terrors of the sinus washout, a less-than-elegant exercise carried out under local anaesthetic. It was customary to see the patients for a follow-up visit a week or so later and pose the question, ‘Are you feeling better, or would you like me to do another washout…?’

We hear much from young surgeons today about how a surgical career would upset their work/life balance. Well, I managed a busy job as a senior registrar and became, after much practice and theoretical study, I became an Associate of the London College of Music. I was doing more performing on the recorder, reviewing concerts for local newspapers, and published my first academic paper, ‘The Crumhorn – an Historical Survey’. I also churned out the required few papers on ENT topics, but really my heart was not in surgical (or indeed medical) research.

Nor was it in head and neck cancer surgery. I have already commented on this aspect of ENT practice, but one abiding memory should be related. I was due to remove the larynx from a woman who had recurrent laryngeal cancer (most laryngectomies were performed on men) and was chatting to her in the anaesthetic room while the anaesthetist prepared his cocktail of drugs. The patient (whose name I cannot recall) held my hand and said, 'I won't be able to talk after I wake up, so I shall talk until I drift off to sleep'. Many years on, I have a 'bell jar memory' of this brief encounter: I'm too sensitive to humanity to be a radical cancer surgeon, but I like to hope that I had other skills in the management of cancer – like palliative care.

During my last year at the REH, one consultant retired early, and another was placed on long-term sick leave, so I was appointed as a locum consultant. This appointment not only increased my responsibility within the REH but also allowed me to pursue my work at the Partial Hearing Units and at a borough audiology clinic which was previously covered by the consultant on sick leave. I was also given a chance to fill a locum consultant slot at the Royal London Homeopathic Hospital in Queen Square. This intrigued me: there was perhaps a higher portion of patients with personality peculiarities that one would find in a conventional ENT clinic, and whilst there, I took the opportunity to sit in with a homeopathic physician in his clinic. Although I did not – and still do not – have any understanding of homeopathy, it was quite clear that these men (most consultants were male in those days!) were very good doctors. They took time to look at social, environmental, and family matters and were clearly treating the whole patient and not just their symptoms. Was it not Michael Balint who wrote, 'The most important prescription a doctor gives is a dose of himself?'

As an aside, I should note that one of the tasks which fall to ENT surgeons is to remove 'foreign bodies' from the nose, throat, and oesophagus.[24] Most of the foreign bodies were fish bones or huge lumps of unchewed food, but all surgeons (I suspect) have their favourite foreign body story, so here is mine. One morning the junior staff asked if I would remove a piece of chicken from a garrulous Glaswegian's oesophagus who told us that he had swallowed the meal on the night train – a very plausible story. However, about 20cm down his oesophagus, I found a blue object (even railway chicken is not blue), and after removing the offending object, I discovered it was part of a neatly-folded matchbox. The patient insisted that he had not eaten a matchbox, so I pointed out that it could hardly have got into his oesophagus any other way and promptly discharged him. It transpired that he had presented on several occasions to different hospitals but with the same story: the man was a classical (and typically sad) example of Munchausen's Syndrome.[25]

Perhaps it is time to deviate from the clinical stuff and look at the administrative side of being an old-fashioned Chief Assistant. The Royal Ear Hospital, a small specialist unit attached to a teaching hospital, although using such facilities as X-ray and pathology in the main hospital, was a very friendly self-contained, and self-administered outfit.

---

[24] The tube leading from the throat to the stomach.

[25] A psychological condition when patients feign illness or injure their bodies to obtain medical attention.

Much of the administrative side was devolved upon the senior registrar, and I had control over the waiting list, admissions, and sorting out the day-to-day problems. On one occasion, I was called to the secretary's office because a man was complaining about the time he had to wait for his operation. I explained that we were only able to operate on urgent cases for a few weeks because the operating theatre lift was being replaced, but he was not really impressed. 'I'm telling you, Doc, that my case is urgent. I've had it for fifteen b….. years'. Hmm. Of particular interest to me was the teaching of medical students, who came to us in groups of six or eight for a month's ENT teaching: I understand that undergraduate experience in the speciality is now about one week… The students – inevitably – exhibited the usual pattern of students everywhere: a few were outstanding, most average, some downright lazy, and not interested in ENT or, for that matter, in the study of any aspect of medicine. Heaven help their future patients. We (the two registrars and I) took our teaching duties very seriously, and in my tenure of the job, the number of applications for the ENT house job went up from about two every six months to twelve: we had great fun with the students, many became friends, and they usually took us out for a beer at the end of their ENT attachment. It was also interesting to teach the housemen the basic ENT operation of tonsillectomy, and it was apparent from their very first attempt at operating those who were potential surgeons and those who most certainly were not. I also had to endure committee meetings; the less said about which, the better.

After four years in post, it was really time to consider my future and look for a permanent senior post as a consultant. I had no great desire nor indeed psychological need to be the boss, and whatever I did, the job had to allow me to pursue my musical interests. I was at the top of the training ladder and was soon to be awarded my Accreditation as a fully-fledged ENT surgeon, but I'm not sure that I endeared myself to the Specialist Advisory Committee on surgical training. This august body chose to inspect the REH and its trainees one Saturday morning, so I was hauled in to be interviewed on my weekend off. I must have had some important musical engagement pending, so I brought in a pile of scores and instrumental parts to edit. The boss opened the door of my office to introduce me to these very senior surgeons, who were, I think, somewhat taken aback to find a not very deferential senior surgical registrar sulking in his room with posters of Renaissance art on the walls and a pile of music on his desk.

So, after three years as a registrar and four and half years as a senior registrar, did I feel ready to be a consultant? Was I confident enough in my operative skills to face anything that was thrown at me? How about the dreaded admin? Certainly, I had absolutely no doubts (nor ever have had) about my diagnostic skills, which I suspect were based on a thorough basic grounding, listening to the patient, and observation, aided by an undefinable 'sixth sense' which has never deserted me. Realistically, I did not want to be a consultant: my secretary at the time observed that I would be dragged screaming into a consultancy! And, of course, I wanted to be a musician and realised that one could be a professional surgeon and a semi-professional musician, but not vice-versa! In my last week at the REH, I passed my Licentiate examination in music so I could face the future as an LLCM as well as an FRCS![26]

I wanted to be in or near the London area and set about looking for a job in the triangle bounded by Guildford, Chichester, and Brighton. Eventually, I found an advertisement for a job as a nine-sessions per week clinical assistant 'with registrar-type duties' at the Royal Surrey County Hospital in Guildford and was duly appointed, principally because of my potential value to the department as an allergist. Needless to say, this rather abrupt change of career path from a consultancy (even if only a locum appointment) at a prestigious London teaching hospital to a very mundane low-ranking post raised a few eyebrows – except amongst those who knew 'how I ticked'. Indeed, one of my fellow senior registrars commented, 'We always thought you would do something like this'.

There is no doubt that it was one of the best decisions I made in my life, although I knew I would miss the REH and

---

[26] Licentiate of the London College of Music.

London life. Instead of the traditional farewell party, I brought a harpsichord into the outpatient department at the REH and, with some friends, gave a farewell concert to the staff before setting off to the provinces in a van packed full of musical instruments. But I did remember to pack my head mirror and stethoscope.

Chapter 11

The next 37 years

Although this book is about my 11 years as a junior doctor, it seems invidious not to conclude with a brief overview of the direction in which my surgical training led.

My post as a clinical assistant was rather mundane, and I do recall writing that I must make of it what I can and 'constructively, be *me*'. Inevitably, as a fully-trained ENT surgeon, these thoughts would lead me away from the conventional tonsil-bashing and the ear-cleaning clinical assistant role, and my first venture was to establish an allergy clinic for nobody in the ENT department (or, as far as I could see, in Guildford) had any experience in this fascinating field: once the local GPs had discovered my existence as an allergist, I was not short of work. Surgically, I was allocated a weekly list of routine procedures and worked a one-in-three on-call with the other clinical assistant and the senior registrar: fortunately, we were not called out frequently, but it was good to be on a one-in-three when the consultants and SHOs were on a one-in-two!

These were the days before 'Macmillan nurses' took over palliative (at that time called terminal) care, and I found myself volunteering for this demanding role, caring for our head and neck cancer patients in their final illness. I think I mentioned earlier that I had been inspired (yes, a word carefully chosen) by the work of Cecily Saunders, and although I may have rattled a few cages by importing her thoughts and methods into the Royal Surrey, I hope I made our patients' final days more comfortable and relatively pain-free.[27]

Music, inevitably, was dominating my existence: my original Renaissance band, the Oriana Consort, transformed itself into a Baroque chamber ensemble, now called Camerata Oriana.

We gave regular concerts in and around Guildford, often with just three or four players, but on occasions extending to a small chamber orchestra supported by a choir: a particular memory is of conducting *Messiah* with eighteen players and singers in aid of the new Princess Alice Hospice at Esher. I built up a small recorder-teaching practice and also taught the recorder one afternoon a week in a boys' prep school: 'Sir, why does a recorder teacher have a stethoscope in his bag?' 'To help him tune his car engine, of course!'.

My other medical fascinations emerged from those Wednesday afternoon 'allergy and calorics' clinics at Barts. After a couple of years, I managed to acquire an extra session in neuro-otology and spent many puzzling hours trying to make sense of dizziness: this can be a very challenging diagnostic puzzle, but the one thing I learnt (and hopefully passed on to my juniors) was that the best diagnostic aid was a comfortable chair for the doctor. With that, one could sit

[27] Dame Cecily used to say that there was not only physical pain, but also mental, social, and spiritual pain.

back and listen: the patient usually gave the answer to the diagnostic puzzle, but *only* if one was prepared to listen. Less messy and less unpleasant than calorics! If I were to have my career over again, I would certainly concentrate on the inner ear, hearing rehabilitation, and balance disorders. These disorders may not be as dramatic as operative surgery, but balance problems are common and usually badly handled in general practice: not, I hasten to say, because of incompetence on the part of the GPs. It's a tricky branch of medicine, and it takes years of training and experience to be even reasonably good at it!

I suppose it is the investigative research temperament (even if in music rather than medicine) that drives me, and allergy can easily become a 'Poirot-esque' exercise. Hay fever is easy enough: take a history, do some simple and safe skin prick tests to confirm the diagnosis, and advise management options: an ENT surgeon, cynical of allergists, once commented that all one had to do to manage allergies was to go on a cruise in the hay fever season, shoot the cat, and burn your feather pillow... The fun really starts with so-called 'food allergies', some of which are real, many of which just represent food sensitivities, and others which comprise an unclassifiable group of people those 'food allergy/sensitivity' can only be viewed with a degree of scepticism. In the 1980s, the real fad was a supposed allergy to yellow colourings in foodstuffs, but, as I understood it, it was impossible for the body to mount a true allergic reaction to these non-protein chemicals. So far, so good – but it was put about that sensitivity (even if not true allergy) to yellow colourings was the cause of multiple educational problems ranging from learning difficulties to uncontrollable bad behaviour. Certainly, there is a small group of people who do get physical symptoms from azo dyes, but the whole thing was exaggerated beyond reason and scientific evaluation – and there were no tests. Surrey is known for its high population of private schools, and it was convenient for the parents who had paid astronomical school fees to blame their beloved offspring's poor school reports on yellow dyes rather than seeking help from an educational psychologist… As far as I know, the yellow food colouring myth has rightly been consigned to history along with the snout masks which doctors wore in the seventeenth century to protect themselves from the plague. Cynically, I am reminded of those who oppose MMR vaccination on the ground of flawed research some years ago and of the Covid 'anti vaxxers' of 2021.

Career-wise, I was appointed to the Associate Specialist grade, giving me permanent senior staff status. Sadly, the grade is now defunct, probably as a result of a typical lack of perception of doctors' needs by those in high medical political positions. Why should it be assumed that all surgeons (or anaesthetists, or physicians, or any other specialists) should want to be consultants? Many suitably qualified practitioners who have other interests, whether that may be in the arts, sport, commerce, or family, do not wish to be burdened with consultant responsibility and just wish to do the job for which they were trained – caring for sick people. Not every teacher aspires to be a head, nor every business person a CEO! I regret the passing of the Associate Specialist grade, for it was a senior and permanent sub-consultant appointment for highly-qualified doctors. There is also a place (which continues) for less-qualified doctors to work as Speciality Doctors, but my long experience in ENT tells me that a line may often be drawn between the Speciality Doctors grade and the former Associate Specialist grade.

I have already commented on how much I enjoyed my perambulations around north London, going to partial hearing units and borough clinics when I was a senior registrar: fortunately, I could continue to escape from the Royal Surrey to attend clinics at Haslemere Hospital and Cranleigh Village Hospital. Both required thirty-minute drives through the Surrey countryside, and lunch usually consisted of a picnic in a suitable beauty spot. The work, of course, was the same, but it was fun to work in different places with different people. Cranleigh was a particular joy: whereas Haslemere had served the local population for years, I established the Cranleigh clinic to care for the locals in Cranleigh, sparing a rather tedious bus journey to Guildford for those without a car. I piggy-backed my idea of a local clinic on the back of Maggie Thatcher's great 'budget holding' scheme: the management was keen to amass revenue from local budget-holding practices, and I was keen to treat the local population… Talking of Haslemere reminds me of a Haslemere lady I treated for many years: she had a narrowing of her throat, and this required dilatation (stretching) every couple of years, and eventually (in ripe old age) she came to her fiftieth (semi-final and successful) dilatation. On the ward round the following morning, I presented her with a small bottle of champagne.

My interest in musical academia was growing, and fired by the enthusiasm of Carl Dolmetsch; I began research into the history of the recorder in the nineteenth century, a period when the instrument was reputed not to exist. After a couple of years' work, I presented my thesis at Trinity College of Music, London, and acquired my second fellowship – now not only FRCS but also FTCL!

As the years rolled on, I became more and more of an ENT physician, and a large proportion of my personal referrals from GPs were for inner ear disorders. At the age of 55, I came off the on-call rota (with a massive sense of relief) and gave up my operating list at 62 in order to do more neuro-otology. In connection with on-call duties, it should be recalled that mobile 'phones only became reliable adjuncts to radio-pagers in the 1990s and that network coverage was patchy, to say the least. Pre-mobiles, we carried radio-pagers, but these only 'buzzed' to indicate that the hospital had to be contacted: the call could be anything from gentle advice to the SHO to an urgent call about a patient about to suffocate from airway obstruction. On-call and off-site, the only way to ensure that one could be instantly available was to note the presence (or absence!) of public telephone boxes and carry a substantial quantity of loose change to feed the things! I was still actively involved in operative surgery during the BSE (bovine spongiform encephalopathy or 'mad cow disease') panic: it was deemed by those in ministerial authority that there was a risk of humans contracting the closely-related Creutzfeldt-Jakob disease in procedures such as tonsillectomy because it was not possible to kill off the responsible prion by standard sterilisation methods. We were accordingly supplied with single-use instruments which were certainly of inferior quality to our standard kit. A disaster: the complication rate of tonsillectomy rose nationally, and I had to abandon my first tonsillectomy using the single-use instruments as the gag used to keep the patient's mouth open would not function satisfactorily. I had to ask the anaesthetist to wake the patient up with his tonsils intact, but this was a safer option than risking his death from uncontrollable bleeding when I had been supplied with inadequate instruments.[28]

At 65, I reduced my commitment to approximately half-time, and at 70, I persuaded the management to allow me to

---

[28] A traditional observation from the aeronautical world reads 'The superior pilot uses his superior judgement to avoid having to using to use his superior skill'. The same applies to operative surgery.

work on one day a week, plus locum cover when needed. The thought of ridiculous and complex revalidation in order to continue working for another few months led to my retirement at 72 – not, as will be seen, to sip coffee in an armchair and watch the telly but to become a full-time (if unpaid!) musicologist.

And what of those final years? I had often expressed the thought that the years between 65 and 70 should be fulfilling after years of experience (and hopefully wisdom) coupled with a lively mind, very perceptive of change, and an ability to care pastorally for staff and patients rather than being a brave and bold surgeon. I became just an ENT physician, taking great delight in caring (yes, in the best sense of the word) for my patients, and during these last years, I reflected that my career had gone through three distinct phases. In the first, I was a young and enthusiastic surgeon wanting to operate on any excuse, but in the second, I became rather unstimulated by the whole exercise. I could do the work without much effort and so deviated very substantially into music, beginning a PhD thesis and also becoming a glider pilot. In my final years, I like to think that I became a doctor in the sense of looking after human beings rather than being totally immersed in operations and medical academia. I also devoted time to caring for our SHOs, for I felt that these young and inexperienced doctors were often at the bottom of the pile for teaching, support, and encouragement. Many of my SHOs became converts to the speciality and are now consultant ENT surgeons: to them; I owe them a debt of gratitude for their constant stimulus and enthusiasm. I was accorded the honour of a Lifetime Achievement Award by the Royal Surrey County Hospital, the citation commenting that I was 'an older statesman and a wise and sound opinion on all aspects of the ENT service'.

Postlude

It has been a good and challenging career: I think that if I had been brought up in a musical family and introduced to music at a much younger age (I only started playing the clarinet at 14), I would probably have become an academic musician, but at least medicine gave me a very adequate salary and pension to devote much of my life and my retirement to music both as a performer and as a researcher. If I were to start a medical career again, I would certainly do ENT and try to avoid a consultancy: inevitably, people ask me, 'would you do medicine again?' My answer is 'if it was now as it was until the 1990s, the answer is yes: if it were to be as now, my answer would be no'. But, all things considered, it was fun!

As has no doubt been obvious, music has been the dominating fascination in my life: since retirement, I have published two books and ten articles in peer-reviewed journals, and although Camerata Oriana has shrunk to Duo Oriana, I continue to perform and have several research projects in progress. Since my school days, I have been stimulated by theological debate, and – despite being intellectually rebellious – I am now a deacon in the Church of England.

The other passion in my life (although probably, in reality, the second after music: surgery is number three!) has been flying. As a boy, I spent many hours honing my handcraft skills-building model aircraft (a valuable exercise in hand/eye co-ordination for the budding surgeon) and still design, build, and fly radio-controlled model gliders. I eventually took up full-sized gliding, and without a doubt, one of the very great moments in my life was my first solo flight: a lifetime ambition finally realised!

But, to conclude, we should return to surgery, for every career must come to an end. At 5.00 pm on Monday, 30 June 2014, I finished my last clinic, walked out of the hospital, and resigned from the medical register at midnight. Five days later, I graduated Doctor of Music at the Royal College of Music, and in October of the same year, I matriculated at St. Cross College, Oxford, to read for the degree of Doctor of Philosophy – inevitably in music…

www.ingramcontent.com/pod-product-compliance
Ingram Content Group UK Ltd.
Pitfield, Milton Keynes, MK11 3LW, UK
UKHW020423250726
13967UKWH00007B/2782

9 781915 662965